# Life Has a Purpose

# Life Has a Purpose

## God's Business Plan for Our Lives

### 5 Basic Principles

Habakkuk 2:2-3

### Dr. Leah Riddick Cunningham

RN, BSN, MCEdu, DHCCEdu

Emotional Health & Wellness Educator

*XULON PRESS*

Xulon Press
2301 Lucien Way #415
Maitland, FL 32751
407.339.4217
www.xulonpress.com

© 2023 by Dr. Leah Riddick Cunningham

All rights reserved solely by the author. The author guarantees all contents are original and do not infringe upon the legal rights of any other person or work. No part of this book may be reproduced in any form without the permission of the author.

Due to the changing nature of the Internet, if there are any web addresses, links, or URLs included in this manuscript, these may have been altered and may no longer be accessible. The views and opinions shared in this book belong solely to the author and do not necessarily reflect those of the publisher. The publisher therefore disclaims responsibility for the views or opinions expressed within the work.

Unless otherwise indicated, Scripture quotations taken from The Message (MSG). Copyright © 1993, 1994, 1995, 1996, 2000, 2001, 2002. Used by permission of NavPress Publishing Group. Used by permission. All rights reserved.

Scripture quotations taken from the Holy Bible, New International Version (NIV). Copyright © 1973, 1978, 1984, 2011 by Biblica, Inc.™. Used by permission. All rights reserved.

Scripture quotations taken from the King James Version (KJV) – *public domain*.

Scripture quotations taken from the Amplified Bible (AMP). Copyright © 1954, 1958, 1962, 1964, 1965, 1987 by The Lockman Foundation. Used by permission. All rights reserved.

Scripture quotations taken from New International Reader's Version (NIRV). Copyright © 1995, 1996, 1998, 2014 by Biblica, Inc.®. Used by permission. All rights reserved worldwide.

Scripture quotations taken from the New English Translation (NET Bible). Copyright ©1996-2006 by Biblical Studies Press, L.L.C. Used by permission. All rights reserved

Paperback ISBN-13: 978-1-66286-123-9
Ebook ISBN-13: 978-1-66286-124-6

*"**LIFE Has a Purpose**" is a great read for all who are seeking their Purpose as well as for people like me, who know their Purpose, but are not walking in the fullness of that Purpose. Dr. Leah and her New Book: "**Life Has a Purpose**" will help you define your heart's Purpose and help you to not let great disappointments, regrets, feeling of failure, hurts, or losses keep you from knowing who God says You are and finding Divine Fulfillment and Purpose!"*

*Pastor, Author Polly Sanders-Peterson*
*Covenant House of Love aka PPS Ministries*

*"**This book helped to renew my commitment to purpose and shed new light on the idea of God's Business Plan for Our Lives.** It is an inspiring read that motivates the reader to act. I'm excited because that action by artists, scientists, teachers, inventors, and careers we have yet to know, can and will change the world."*

*Actress, Angela Robinson*
*'The Haves and Have Nots'*

*"**Throughout the manuscript, the author is very insightful, honest, and encouraging. She poses fantastic rhetorical questions that are a catalyst for deeper thinking and reflection on the reader's part about the greater schemes of life.** Further, the author includes great figurative language, specifically metaphors, to get through to readers and paint them a picture that furthers her point. Inclusion of the author's own personal experiences is wonderful!"*

*Xulon Press Christian Publishing*

*Two things you can never get back:*

*Yesterday and all "its" regrets*

*Live well today*

*Because . . .*

Life *Has* a Purpose

# *A Personal Note*

There was a time when I was losing and reclaiming my life at the same time, but I didn't know it.

**2017**

I had just purchased my $250K home. Then five months later, my six-figure salary job gave me an ultimatum, so we parted ways.

My place of worship for greater than twenty-five-plus years, where I served faithfully, was no longer available to me.

My savings and assets that I never concerned myself about were dwindling down like a man whittling a stick.

My personal life had become a lonely place, and I had to learn to love my own company all over again.

**2018**

Everything I had come to rely on was disappearing like a poor magic trick, yet, God was sustaining me.

Then, with the little money I had, God required me to throw *Him* a party, and I had my first and very successful conference called "Embrace You, With No Apologies." It wasn't until later that I realized that conference was required by God, but it was about and for me.

I received a prophecy at that conference, and God told me, "Before you have your next conference, you will be married." Though I was glad to hear it, I silently scoffed. I had heard it all before, too many times to count.

The year was coming to a close, and so were my hopes and dreams. I wasn't sure what would happen next.

**2019**

> I became employed again.
> I served in a church again.
> I started dating again.
> I even married again.
> I was fulfilled again.

My life *does* have a purpose, and in these pages, you will discover that yours does too!

# *Dedication*

I dedicate this book to my husband, Rayland. He has been my source of encouragement and motivation to finish this book.

When we met, I had been working on this book for two years. He believed in me, my ministry, and the love I have for and to obey God.

Rayland was the one who had the vision for the renaissance of my ministry from the ministry I had before him to what it has become with him.

He is my life partner, business manager, executive director, best friend, and Ephesians 5 husband.

He is and will forever be my hero and king!

I dedicate this book to him.

# Contents

*Part 1*
*Purpose*

Introduction . . . . . . . . . . . . . . . . . . . . . . . . . . . . . . . . . . . . . . . . . . xix
1. . . . . . . . . . . . .Who Am I? . . . . . . . . . . . . . . . . . . . . . . . . . . . . . . . . . .11
2. . . . . . . . . . . . .Where Do I Belong?. . . . . . . . . . . . . . . . . . . . . . . . . . . .15
3. . . . . . . . . . . . .When Do I Feel Fulfilled? . . . . . . . . . . . . . . . . . . . . . 19
4. . . . . . . . . . . . .Why Do I Feel Frustrated? . . . . . . . . . . . . . . . . . . . . .23

*Part 2*
*God's Business Plan for Our Lives*
Habakkuk 2:2–3

5. . . . . . . . . . . . Discovering God's Business Plan . . . . . . . . . . . . . . . . . 29
6. . . . . . . . . . . . Principle 1—See It. . . . . . . . . . . . . . . . . . . . . . . . . . . .31
7. . . . . . . . . . . . Principle 2—Write It. . . . . . . . . . . . . . . . . . . . . . . . . 49
8. . . . . . . . . . . . Principle 3—Read It, Run with It . . . . . . . . . . . . . . . . . 59
9. . . . . . . . . . . .Principle 4—Wait for It . . . . . . . . . . . . . . . . . . . . . . . .67
10. . . . . . . . . . . . Principle 5—Be It. . . . . . . . . . . . . . . . . . . . . . . . . . . .85

Conclusion: *Purpose* Is Fulfillment . . . . . . . . . . . . . . . . . . . . . . . 89
Meet the Author . . . . . . . . . . . . . . . . . . . . . . . . . . . . . . . . . . . . . .91
References . . . . . . . . . . . . . . . . . . . . . . . . . . . . . . . . . . . . . . . . .93

# *Foreword*

*I*was in Jacksonville, FL enjoying an acting career at a local theatre, teaching Modeling at a local school and mentoring youth. I knew there was something more but I did not know what to do to get it. One day I fell to my knees asking God for direction and he (through my pastor) led me to a book by the late Miles Munroe called In Pursuit of Purpose. That book changed my life. I knew that my desires were not mere pipe dreams but indeed a part of my divine purpose. **Dr. Cunningham's Life Has a Purpose is an on-time word! Reading it took me back but also propelled me forward. She takes principles on purpose to a new level. This book helped to renew my commitment to purpose and shed new light on the idea of God's Business Plan for Our Lives.** It is an inspiring read that motivates the reader to act. I'm excited because that action by artists, scientists, teachers, inventors, and careers we have yet to know, can and will change the world.

*Angela Robinson, Actress*

Angela Robinson, Actress, *"The Haves and Have Nots"*
Leah Riddick Cunningham, Author

# *Introduction*

I wish to liken *Life Has a Purpose* to a comparison of basic steps in a simplistic business plan. A business plan should be strategically written for the purpose of outlining each step of an idea as a "business model" that will lead to a successful and profitable venture. The goal is to present a map that allows to you navigate through terrain and territories you have never explored before. Some areas you will skillfully avoid. Others, maybe not so much! But because you have a plan and a map, you can reach your destination.

Regardless of how well any business plan is written, you will experience unpredictable events. Because *this* business plan is called life, *it* will happen; it's just a matter of when.

Let's look at two basic yet quintessential parts of a business plan, the two areas that can swiftly tell you if this is a worthwhile venture.

**The Introduction and the Executive Summary**

An introduction briefly explains what the document is about and may contain your goals and objectives.

An executive summary is a condensed version of the entire report and can be read as a standalone document.

What can someone tell about your life? Does your life represent an introduction or the executive summary?

Let's look at how each are defined.

The introduction is the first section of the document. It explains what the document is about and why you have written it. The introduction merely sets the scene. The introduction to the document is like the first ten minutes of a movie in which you obtain a vague preview of what the story is going to be about.

You cannot understand what the entire business plan is about simply by reading the introduction. When we live our lives without purpose it's very much just an introduction, a snapshot of what we are supposed to be. We cannot nor should we try to conclude who we are without having a clear understanding of our purpose.

The executive summary, which can be twenty to thirty pages or more, is the full document of our life's purpose—including the many years of living—condensed to a few bullet points or paragraphs, reflecting our passion and commitment to our purpose![1]

You should be able to get the gist of the entire document, who we are, simply by reading the executive summary. The executive summary *is* the entire movie script condensed to a few short paragraphs. One has to understand that this extremely condensed version of our lives is a foretelling of the most important aspects of *us*, and it makes the case about why the subject matter, what our lives offer, is relevant.

That's why it is necessary to ask yourself, if your life is written as a business plan, who should write it? You?

No!

Though the executive summary is often at the beginning of a document, some writers benefit from writing it last. This allows the writer to thoroughly develop *all* their conclusions and arguments during the other stages of the writing process and simply focus on summarizing and persuading in the executive summary, and for some, that is okay.

But who is the *only* one qualified to write your life as a business plan and include *everything* about your life that will *ever* happen—at the *beginning* of your life, the good, the bad, and the indifferent—*and* still make it a good investment? God!

The unfortunate thing for us is that we aren't aware that our lives are basically already designed as a great investment and that we are living a business plan written by God waiting to be put into operation and make our contribution to the world through our purpose. Many have spent a lot of wasted time seeking, searching, and hunting to find their purpose when we never really needed to look for it; we only needed to tap into it. Purpose is to be discovered within, not without.

Cease to look anywhere further than within you as I help you discover your "not-so-hidden" purpose.

It's been waiting on you to find it because the world is waiting on you to *surrender* it.

Life *has* a purpose!

# *Purpose*

*Defined by Oxford is simply this—*
(n) the reason for which something is done or created or for which something exists.[2]

*You're here to bear fruit, reproduce, lavish life on the Earth, live bountifully!* (Gen. 9:7 MSG)

# *Part 1*

# *Purpose*

---

**Don't Let Life Just Happen to You**

"Life, is what happens to us while we are making other plans,"[3] is a quote written by John Allen Saunders. This was published in Reader's Digest in January 1957, when John Lennon was seventeen. Many have believed John Lennon to be the author of this famous quote. His quote is a slight variation, "Life is what happens to you while *you're busy* making other plans."[4] Lennon's modest revision reflects a paradox in our lives. Many of us would like to have a peaceful ride and enjoy the present moment, yet we can't help but make future plans so we feel secure, or we spend time digging on past hurts.

We must look at why this quote implies a paradox in our lives. When we define a *paradox life*, we are discussing an inconsistent life, a life not sure, a life of absurdities. But at the same time, we are actively making plans in an attempt to avoid the same. Thus, while we are planning life, life is evidently happening to us, leaving us to hope that it ultimately is happening for our good, somehow, some way!

**As you *live,* you might as well enjoy *life* and fulfill your life's purpose.**

Now, I know that sounds a bit confusing, perhaps may be a little trite, but it's true! Because the understanding is that *life* is different from *live*. Human beings' existence is simply defined by the fact that we live, breathe, eat, sleep, think, and, therefore, we are! Right? But we also, as human beings, have the unique ability to reason through intellect. But the maximum potential of the human body, soul, and spirit as a whole is *under-utilized* because many people don't really live; we just exist! We take up space! Do you know a piece of fruit does that, simply take up space? Hmm . . . that is not my idea of life.

**Let's look at a biblical reference of what makes human beings unique and special creations of God?**

Holman Bible Publishers (Copyright c 1991) "Image of God" biblical description, made some references of human's being special creations of God in the following manner, "According to the Scriptures, humans are not an evolutionary accident but a special creation. Human beings were *purposefully* created by God to fulfill a preordained role in His world. We have peculiar qualities that reflect the nature of God Himself, and these set us apart and above all other created beings.

Humans created in God's image share His rational nature. We have the power to think, analyze, and reflect even upon abstract matters. We cannot be defined by or confined to material attributes. As God is spiritual\* (John 4:24), persons are spiritual. This spiritual kinship makes possible communication with God.

**The Bible teaches that human beings have purpose.**

Humans have an *instinctive* need to be something and to do something. They have a responsible intuition and an inner call to duty. The human race has a unique sense of "oughtness." Humans are moral creatures. \*\* They can and do make moral judgments. People have a censoring conscience, which they may defy. They are choice makers; they can obey their highest instincts or follow their most morbid urges. A human is the only creature who can say no to God. Humans are autonomous persons. God endowed them with the freedom to govern their own lives."[5]

\* *"God is spirit, and his worshipers must worship in the Spirit and in truth"* (John 4:24 NIV).

\*\* *"You may freely [unconditionally] eat [the fruit] from every tree of the garden; but [only] from the tree of the knowledge [recognition] of good and evil you shall not eat"* (Gen. 2:16–17 MSG).

This understanding of our nature is why life can often seem like a paradox because we have the ability to search for the good in life through intellect and reason. In doing so, when life hits us with the undesirable, uncertainties, dislikes, unpleasantries, and the like *without our permission*, it becomes detrimental to many of us. Disappointments and challenges have the ability to shatter everything we know as life. In actuality, it's like someone shutting down our lives. It's devastating.

Life becomes contrary to everything the Scriptures promise us. *"I am come that they might have life, and that they might have it more abundantly"* (John 10:10 KJV). Let's focus on the operative word, *abundant*, which according to Merriam Webster Dictionary, means "existing or occurring in large amounts: ample, *plentiful in everything*!" This understanding about life is significantly different from just living, just taking up space! Unfortunately, many people don't know how to do more with their lives. Consequently, we then live our lives beneath our purpose and are in a constant vicious cycle of looking *externally* for more. We are looking for our purpose.

**Our Life's Purpose Evolves**

Sharon Daloz Parks, who studied theology at Harvard Divinity School, states, "questions about your life's purpose may arise at any time in life, but you may notice that they are especially prevalent during times of transition or crisis, such as a career or educational change, personal loss, long-distance move, or a separation of relationships. Daloz Parks, calls these events "life's shipwrecks."[6]

Our lives should never be characterized by one event, relationship, career, accomplishment, or even failure. Our life's purpose continues to evolve into the next chapter of our lives. Just as the earth's yearly calendar has seasons of change, so do we. We have growth and development throughout our life span, from infancy to adulthood. Let's review it for a minute. As human beings, we will commonly experience seven stages of life to include infancy, early childhood, middle childhood, adolescence, early adulthood, middle adulthood, and old age. So it is with life's purpose. We grow and develop into each new stage of our lives, and in doing so, we *evolve* into our lives and thus evolve into our purpose. Can you imagine concluding our purpose in childhood or, more alarmingly, during adolescence, a time in which a big part of our living, learning, and understanding is quantified by our peers? Yikes!

We should recognize that in many areas of our lives, such as our financial evolution, educational evolution, spiritual evolution and ultimately evolution of our life's purpose, that if we choose not to believe in continuous evolution of life's purpose, by *default,* we are believing we become the only *one* thing we ever experience, whether good, bad, or indifferent! I shudder to think of some of the things that I experienced that didn't go well and the possibility of being stuck with that experience labeling me for the rest of my life. Thank God that is not the case!

Let's look at a story of the goldfish and the fish bowl. Is the following a myth or truth? Whenever you take a goldfish from a small fishbowl and place it in a larger one, do you know it will grow to that size? *True!* It will *evolve* into the space that has been provided, and it will adapt there and exist well. In the same way, if you keep a goldfish in the same small size fishing bowl all of its life, it will remain that size. It will stop evolving or growing, retain the small purpose or function in life it has adapted to, and live out its existence as a small goldfish, and, in essence, it will never reach its full potential. Its life's purpose is limited by a lack of opportunity.

Let's stay here just for another moment.

'Cosmos and The Science of Everything', on September 19, 2016, wrote an article entitled "Do Goldfish Really Grow to the Size of Their Tank."[7] This is an interesting fact that we will explore. Goldfish produce a growth-inhibiting hormone (GIH) that builds up in the water. When that water is changed all the time, the hormone is removed, and the fish continues to grow. A bigger tank helps to dilute this hormone, which is why goldfish tend to get really big in big tanks.

Conversely, in a small bowl or tank, the GIH is very concentrated, having more ability to inhibit growth. Without any way for the GIH to become diluted, the fish's growth becomes inhibited by the lack of proper conditions of its own environment.

Therefore, we conclude that small goldfish are only small because they are environmentally stunted.

In these smaller fish bowls or in aquariums with poor water quality and improper care, the stunting that results are a sign of ill health, and frequently, stunted fish take on a deformed appearance and die at a young age. Wow, who knew?

Let's view the plight of this goldfish as a metaphor for people who are never placed in an environment where they can flourish; they will become ill, dwarfed in their purpose, and die without ever reaching fulfillment. However, if there was a *paradigm shift,* and we learned to realize life's poor experiences should not be allowed to become our "be all end all," we could allow ourselves to evolve in life, and our gifts, talents, and influence could be identified, cultivated, utilized, and brought to maturation and so evolve into a purpose for our lives. There it is clarification through development! People just need the right environment; they need to be often provided with fresh, clean water and cared for properly, and they will grow! Given proper care and conditions, the evolution of our purpose is basically guaranteed!

How interesting that the symbol of a fish is symbolic of identifying Christians. I get it. Do you?

**Purpose Consists of a Multiplicity of Reasons**

Your life's purpose reflects the multiplicity of reasons why you get up in the morning! Our daily lives reflect many physical efforts, including the vast skills some possess to acquire the greater material things of life, the complex knowledge to gain great wealth, or the corporate know-how of how to quickly climb the corporate ladder. These common exercises of life have their place, but they can be exhausting, mundane, superficial, and breed impulsivity; not to mention that, for some, the goal of earthly success is often subject to being unachievable due to the many unforeseen earthly factors of life. Life's purpose shouldn't only involve elements, such as your career, where you live, or what you own; these are so provisional. On the contrary, life should indeed include a spiritual purpose, and establishing a set of values, principles, and beliefs that give life meaning to you, and then using them to guide the decisions and actions you take, which typically will involve others.

Purpose is unique for everyone. It guides our decisions, influences behavior, creates goals, and helps you identify your path or journey in life. Purpose is what gives your life meaning as it relates to the essence of why you are here! This should be and will be different from everyone else you know, even though there will be hints and even profound similarities to others and their lives' purpose. Just as human beings are composed of millions of cells and molecules that create our DNA, though it will never create the *exactness* of one human in another, likewise our purpose should never be imagined to be like anyone else's. It is not only okay to choose a different path of your purpose, but if a path does not yet exist, it's okay to *create* it!

Realize as life evolves, so does purpose!

Some areas of reflection as you read this book to discover your life's purpose are:

*Purpose*

- Who am I?
- Where do I belong?
- When do I feel fulfilled?
- Why do I feel frustrated?
- What steps can I take to discover my purpose?

This reflection should lead you to this poignant reality:

*Life* has a purpose, which is becoming the *best* version of you, so that you live your life with the *intent* to live your life that it may impact others for the *better*!

# One

# *Who Am I?*

---

Our purpose should always follow first from knowing who we are. It is important to accept the truth that we are "fearfully and wonderfully made" (Ps. 139:14 NIV) and that we are created in the image and likeness of God (Gen. 1:26 NIV). This might create an image of a blank, fresh canvas we will call life, and life just waiting for creativity and purpose to arise within us. This should be achieved through emulation because God himself is a creator with no limits . . . but let's get there.

When we take a moment to review our own existence, we would have to realize that we came from a source that wasn't already here, for instance, a human egg cell and a human sperm cell. Now, this is simplistic, but it bears enough value to have a discussion. An egg comes from the mother; she produces it, and the sperm comes from the father; he produces it, and the union of the two, the conception of the two, *produces* you. We then are considered products of the combination of these two substances. Simple. Often, you will hear people say, "You look just like your dad" or "You have your mom's eyes." Some might even mention a resemblance as far back as noting how you share a feature of your grandparents. Of course, this may not be true for all. Some may say they don't have any true resemblance or features of their natural parents, and they wouldn't be wrong. But, perhaps, if we look closer, we will discover that they share similarities of likes and dislikes, mannerisms, manners of speech, and certain entertainment and sport interests; maybe they followed the same path of work, trades, college majors, adventures, entrepreneurship ventures, skills, or life goals.

All things being created equal, we would certainly expect that there would be some quality or characteristic that suggests a family connection, the thing that makes people say, "Oh yeah, I see now that you certainly are your daddy's little girl" or "your mother's son." When people first meet you, and they say, "I think I know you . . . you are from the Miller family, right?" something exudes from you that, in essence, gives you away.

The truth is that you are a byproduct of whoever created you, and that has produced something within you resembling the family connection, however big or small, conspicuous or inconspicuous, and even pleasant or repugnant. Even if there was nothing else that showed evidence of the family connection, shouldn't knowing the one who created you satisfy you enough to know that you are a part of the family? Some may suggest that yes, it should. But we know that contrary to popular belief, "One size *doesn't* fit all." So, let's go deeper.

**Identity**

If we are discussing our first point of reflection— "Who am I?"— we can make an association of characteristics, looks, similar interests, and so on as we've discussed, though this is not going to hold true in all instances because everything is not visible or easily detectable. So, there must be more.

Yes, there is! We have a unique pattern of cells that are an inheritable quality, our fingerprints. Given to us by our parents, they can't be seen, no one easily notices them, nor do they come up in discussion when people are trying to associate us within our families. These patterns are often genetically inherited, but the individual details that make a fingerprint unique are not. In a January 4, 2005 article of *Scientific American* it was noted that "Friction ridge skin (FRS) covering the surfaces of their hands and feet are what make the impressions on our fingertips, toes, and feet."[8] When we come into the world, as byproducts of our parents, if we are born in hospitals, they will take our footprints after birth. It identifies you. The mother's fingerprints are taken and recorded with the newborn's footprints for reliable identification records. The newborn's footprints, along with the mother's fingerprints, become part of the hospital's records as a requirement by states to help prevent mix-ups in hospital nurseries. The FRS is unique and permanent, and no two individuals (including identical twins) have the same. Moreover, the arrangement of the ridges and features do not change throughout our lifetime, with the exception of significant damage that creates a permanent scar. Therefore, each person's fingerprints are unique, which is why they have long been used as a way to identify individuals. Like many other complex traits, studies indicate that both genetic and environmental factors play a role in the development of these unique patterns. The same article stated, "It has been demonstrated that you are more likely to share a pattern type with your family members than with an unrelated individual, but your identifying FRS features will always be unique to you." Identity!

But the larger question of "Who am I?" should not be an inquiry that people only limit to questions about themselves regarding our natural family relationships, but it is more important to ask it about our spiritual relationships. Like our fingerprints, even if we don't visibly see the connection to our natural family, we now know our fingerprints or footprints at birth connect us anyway. Similarly, our current lifestyles may not resemble that of our spiritual parent, the source of all creation, yet we are and always will be created from a source greater than us. And our life's purpose is already deposited in us from birth by the one who created us. Who am I? Well, you are your Father's child!

The Great I Am having already deposited our purpose; our purpose is waiting on our discovery.

# Two

# *Where Do I Belong?*

*Y*our life's purpose is your life's contribution. Wherever your contribution serves best should be an indicator of where you'll find you belong! True purpose is about recognizing your own gifts or influence and using them to contribute to the world. We will use contribution and influence interchangeably to make our point.

Gifts can be known as any of the following: music, dancing, writing, helping, serving, educating, ministering, singing, donating, caring, giving, nursing, doctoring, painting, building, encouraging, healing, protecting, providing, and creating, and even the ability to bring joy, love, happiness, peace, tranquility, and so much more into someone's life can be a gift. Whatever they may be, your gifts are the source of your influence over others for the greater good. When you authenticate your gift by using it for the good of others, your purpose becomes clear, and you have a burning desire to share it.

Belonging can be a matter of philosophical debate, with many metaphors and analogies to support each argument. The *Merriam-Webster Dictionary* describes the word *belong* as an intransitive verb.[9] The meaning that fits best here is: "(3) to be an attribute, part, adjunct, or function of a person or thing, *i.e.,* nuts and bolts *belong* to a car."

Our *gifts* are the equivalence of our being a contribution to something, someone, or someplace. The significance is the necessity of the contribution. Just like the car is in need of the nuts and bolts for the car to be considered safe, reliable, functional, and even be known as a *car,* it *requires* the nuts and bolts. In other words, the parts that make up a car are not optional; they are mandatory. The entire car is not, nor will it be, what it was designed to be *without* the nuts and bolts. Consequently, we belong where our gift or influence fits best to the point that without our influence, the thing or place or person would malfunction.

It would be safe to say that many contributions given as gifts should make anything better, especially financial gifts. Many people are accustomed to contributions being associated with finances or donations to a cause or charity. These are monetary contributions. Commonly, monetary contributions have a way of bringing an almost immediate reward of some type to the contributor. We understand money to be considered a currency. A currency is a medium of exchange for goods and services.[10] The operative word is *exchange*. This implies that there is an expectation of a gain or something in return. But it would be unhealthy to associate that statement as an answer to the question, "Where do I belong?" since it reflects an *immediate* exchange of getting something in return.

When you feel a desire or hunger deep within to offer your gifts to a person, place, or thing, it should be such an overwhelming feeling that it becomes unquenchable until you give it away. It's like love in that way. It is understood by most that love isn't love until it is freely given away. Love can't be fulfilled or considered complete in its purpose if you are the only one who possesses it. By giving it away, your love comes full circle.

The same is true of your gift, your influence. Sharing any gift— whether it is a gift that is non-tangible like a service, or one that is tangible like a thing or item—brings about a release of emotions that floods your mind and body, like an activation of dopamine. Dopamine is the body's natural chemical release of our "happy place or pleasure" sense. Giving our gifts away makes us feel happy and fulfilled. It allows us to feel that we belong because we've provided for a need. Nothing else typically is needed. The gift wasn't given for gain; it was given to make a difference. The sense of belonging is fundamental to the way humankind organizes itself. No man is an island; that is not how we were created to live, nor could we survive long independently of one another.

Let's put all of this into context. When we wonder where we belong, we belong where we can *give* our gift away or use our influence freely, without a *need* for reward, accolades, recognition, or self-gain.

Giving our gifts solely *fulfills us* as we *empty ourselves of it*. In fact, it would be safe to say that until you arrived, there was a lack, a void, a missing piece to someone, something, or someplace. Your gift or influence was the only thing that had the capacity to fill that missing need. When you provided for it, you were fulfilled.

So, let's understand that our longing for belonging is fulfilled by contributing our gifts, our influence, which then allows you to define your purpose. What you contribute is what connects you, and what connects you is what fulfills you!

# Three

# *When Do I Feel Fulfilled?*

This one is relatively simple. In my opinion, many behaviorists commonly would say fulfillment is self-actualization. In psychology, self-actualization is achieved when you're able to reach your *full* potential. That most certainly has a ring of truth to it. I would not discount this meaning.

Additionally, we have already established that fulfillment runs tandem with belonging and connecting. It's where you discover how you can best contribute your gift and operate in your sphere of influence for the better good of someone else. Being truly self-actualized, therefore, is considered the exception rather than the rule since most people are working on what they have determined to be more important needs.

When one comes into an understanding of their gifts, their influence, and recognizes that it allows them to solve a problem for someone else, something else, or another place, it provides fulfillment. It causes you to acknowledge someone else's need. You deem yourself as not as needy as the other, even though you may also be in want. However, this exception allows you to see other people's need as a priority, not yourself.

This is not the norm.

It is the nature of many people to be selfish. Selfishness is the tendency to prioritize one's own desires and needs above the needs and desires of other people.[11] If you step back from this phrase, you can almost see its significance. It is believed that most Americans, if asked about their priorities in life, they would be to live in good health, have a roof over their head, lead a happy life, have enough money to live comfortably, and enjoy a good family life. And they wouldn't necessarily be wrong for wanting these things. Heck, I want that too! But the difference is how you go about obtaining it, your pursuit of it. How have you prioritized this list of American dreams, and what is your method of obtaining it? This is where we often run into issues.

The pursuit of American dreams of this type often leads us into a mode of living that is completely contradictory to understanding that life has a purpose in the context of what we have identified thus far. In fact, the single-minded pursuit of our dreams often becomes so opposite of the idea of influence that its definition, as we read below, can be considered very dark.

The *Merriam-Webster Dictionary* has defined *selfishness* as: "concerned excessively or exclusively with oneself; seeking or concentrating on one's own advantage, pleasure, or well-being *without regard for others.*" Yikes, having no regard for anyone else! We hear about that more often than we would care to admit in our daily lives.

Fulfillment is solving a problem for someone over solving yours *first*. This is not the norm.

This understanding causes us to evaluate that century-old question of *Why am I here*? We may have often thought it was just to satisfy ourselves: make money, have nice homes, live comfortably, be as healthy as you can be, have happy families and good jobs, yada, yada, yada . . . right? In reality, we never master that 100 percent of the time because there will most likely be something out of *rhythm* with our pursuit of that American-made cycle of achievement, where those things are never all in sync at the same time. And, in the rare moments when they all are in sync, does it ever last as long as we feel it should? This cycle of pursuit then sends us back searching for purpose again because those short-term efforts and accomplishments, though noteworthy, are never life-long sustaining. They're just temporary, seasonal, merely defined only by life's next happy occasion, not life's purpose or fulfillment.

So, then the single-minded pursuit of our dreams potentially *never* results in really reaching our God-given purpose because one of those personal dreams would always be unobtainable to the point that it never brings us the fulfillment we seek.

May I then suggest, in fact, reiterate that we are here for something more, for some other reason and someone else and their need? In fact, let us *agree* our purpose in life is to provide for a need!

When we revisit the list of questions to ponder in chapter two, which makes mention of some of our many talents, gifts, and ability to be influential, let's admit: who *typically* gets the *most* benefit and pleasure out of giving . . . someone else, right? Who gets the most *reward* from it . . . we do!

It is here where purpose becomes unmistakably and undoubtedly what it is supposed to be in your life. It is the moment when someone else's need has become fulfilled by your existence. Your purpose becomes clear when the inability to reach their own capacity becomes met. Thus, your unselfish expression of your best self has been serving someone else.

Ladies and gentlemen, may I introduce to some and enlighten others about "the purpose of life!"

I'm living to add to someone else's life, and I will get the biggest reward from doing so. Consequently, someone else is living for me, and I will get the biggest benefit and pleasure from their contribution to my life.

**Therefore, it becomes imperative for each of us to search within, not without, for our purpose.**

This should cause us to evaluate our purpose internally, intentionally, and inherently. It was deposited within us at birth. We can't go to school to obtain it, only perhaps cultivate it. We can't lose it, only misuse it through ignorance; we can't even sell it because only your DNA can authenticate it and its identity in you.

It certainly can't be measured by only what we do, for what we do, through gifts and influence that can't ever really be measured. Never try to measure capacity by contribution but rather by lack.

*We ourselves feel that what we are doing is just a drop in the ocean. But the ocean would be less because of that missing drop.*

*— Mother Teresa*

# Four

## *Why Do I Feel Frustrated?*

---

As we are discovering, fulfillment in life is not found through the mediocre activities of life or events but purpose. If purpose is measured by anything other than real fulfillment, by default, one can easily become frustrated.

The pursuit of fulfillment becomes frustrating because some of our activities and pursuit of life can be orchestrated by other people—either by family traditions or the expectations of others—and as we try to oblige others by fulfilling their purpose, through our lives, without regard to our own fulfillment, the pursuit of fulfillment most definitely will result in frustration.

Additionally, not knowing our true purpose or being able to identify our gifts or sphere of influence also adds to frustration. Any one of these components or all of them is easily a recipe for frustration. When there is no real source of fulfilling purpose that leaps within you, the search for fulfillment can do just the opposite. It can leave you empty, hollow, and even feeling useless. One can easily become bitter, discouraged. and disappointed with life. Everyone wants to feel needed. Purpose allows us to fill a need.

Long-term frustration can even be a deterrent to dedicating more time to ultimately seeking out your true purpose. One's search becomes an exercise in futility. Concentrated efforts of a search that doesn't yield any fruit can be the epitome of frustration, frustration then can be characterized as an emotion that occurs in situations where a person is blocked from reaching a desired outcome. In general, whenever we reach one of our goals, we feel pleased, and whenever we are *prevented* from reaching our goals, we may succumb to frustration and feel irritable, annoyed, and angry. Typically, the more important the goal, the greater the frustration, which results in anger or loss of confidence. Our goal is finding our life's purpose.

A frustrated life can be so detrimental to one's self that we begin to see behaviors that are counterintuitive to a healthy lifestyle or becoming a positive contributor member of society. Some behaviors exhibit themselves as becoming angry and wanting to give up or quit. One may begin to lose their self-esteem, loss of self-confidence, experience stress, sadness, depression, anxiety, and even worst, turn to substance abuse.

I define frustration as *emotional depletion*. A depleted emotional life sets us on a course of self- destruction, sometimes even unbeknownst to us. We begin to make choices that are inappropriate, immoral, and even unethical, to name a few. We may develop characteristics that are unknown to us. One can begin to spiral downward out of frustration. Even the worst of fears could be realized due to frustration, and one may decide to resign themselves from life. This is why we must discard the notion that merely performance of any job will dictate our inner calling, gifts, and more specifically our purpose. This would be better known as merely a perfunctory duty, not a calling, and it is most certainly not fulfilling.

It is encumbered upon everyone to seek out their true purpose in life because there is so much more to life than what we may merely do. Some of us are holding space while we follow up on where we belong, what connects us, and what fulfills us.

Our purpose supplies so many needs for so many others; it really does become a quite fulfilling life of great rewards. Achieving our purpose is not limited by our use but rather our lack of effort. Don't refrain from exercising your gifts or operating in your sphere of influence; it is a gift to someone.

Let us not withhold ourselves from what we have to give because our hope is that the person who is supposed to share their gift with us will not do the same.

*Yesterday is gone. Tomorrow has not yet come. We have only today. Let us begin.*

—*Mother Teresa*

# Part 2

## God's Business Plan for Our Lives

*Habakkuk 2:2-3*

# Five

## *Discovering God's Business Plan*

---

Come with me as I discuss the simple principles of discovering your inner purpose. God's Word gives us instructions on everything.

The following principles of how to have a plan for your life will allow you to evolve into your life's purpose of achieving many accomplishments, multiple goals, a myriad of success, and a plethora of happiness all in one lifetime!

Who said you can't have it all while you're here . . . of course, you can! Your "life has a purpose"!

Life should not be what happens to you but rather what happens for you! Yes, we get it, that a big part of life is what happens while we are making plans . . . it's that, all *of a sudden,* here comes the unexpected called life. Yes, been there, done that, bought the T-shirt! However, whatever that unexpected moment of life was, it still doesn't get to become my whole life. Life's focus should be what happens *for* us.

The biggest way to navigate from what happens *to* us in life to what happens *for* us is to have a plan for your life! Why? How would that benefit someone if what happens to us is the unexpected? Simply put, a plan gives you something to re-route *from.* It gives you something to work from as you are working toward something better! You have to have been heading somewhere, attempting to accomplish something, and seeking to become someone.

One of my most admired quotes comes from Eleanor Roosevelt, who said, "No one can make you feel inferior without your consent." How true is that! You have the last say about you and your life. Other people's actions, commentary, or opinions can't be stopped from being done or said, but you can sure stop it from having any effect on your life! The criticism of others can only have input or effectiveness if you allow it to. By the same token, no one can make you feel inferior about your life's errors, flaws, mistakes, mis-steps, or mis-haps unless you allow it—in other words, unless you *agree*! Even in the most stressful and dreadful times, the decision is up to you because it's only when you decide, "Okay, that's enough," does that moment in life become enough. And once you've said that to yourself, life has just shifted in your favor.

Life is way too short to just let it happen. You have to plan in life.

Life has a purpose!

# Six

# *Principle 1—See It*

## *—Habakkuk 2:2 AMP*

---

'Vision-you must *see* something to create something, and, if it doesn't exist, then you must *imagine* it.'

Ordinarily to see something, one must have a certain amount of vision. However, this chapter is where we will discuss 'see it' as a correlated understanding of vision, but not necessarily eyesight. My perspective comes from the research found in Bible Tools, *Greek/Hebrew Definitions*, where the meaning for the word *vision* is "mental sight."[12] Let us agree that the word *mental* would imply this vision comes from within us, not from outside of us. This is to indicate that the "mental sight" refers to our "mind's eye" and not our physical eyesight. But allow me to explain.

I am going to take you through a quick easy review of Visual Acuity 101 to make my point.

Let's review the following:

> Medline Plus, *Medical Encyclopedia* describes normal visual acuity, as measured by a Snellen chart, is 20/20[13]. Meaning, the average person with healthy vision should be able to read the chart at a distance of twenty feet.

This would signify that this person is sharp-sighted; they have sharpness of vision with the ability to resolve fine detail as measured by the use of a Snellen chart. Simplified further, this person has the ability to see and read what is twenty feet in front of them. This level of vision, the manner in which one sees or conceives of something, is known as normal eyesight.

What is necessary for this to take place are a few basic yet obvious human vision components: the eye itself, the visual center in the brain, and the optic nerve, which connects the two. Stay with me. I'm going somewhere.

The eye operates like a camera. Light rays enter through the adjustable iris of the eye and are focused by the lens onto the retina at the back of the eye. The retina converts the light into nerve impulses, which are relayed to the visual center. There, the brain *interprets* the nerve impulses as images. Ahh, I *see* (sorry, couldn't resist)! But, let's continue.

Why do you need to know this? With this statement being true about our normal visual acuity aka "20/20 eyesight," what would be true of those who don't have normal visual acuity? Let's explore that for a moment.

Some people have impaired vision for many reasons. For the purpose of this section, we will discuss only three very common ones. I have simplified the medical definitions.

1) Farsightedness: *Hyperopia* [hi-per-o´pe-ah]—a defect of vision, where one's vision is better for distant objects than for near.[14]
2) Nearsightedness: *Myopia* [mi-o´pe-ah]—a defect of vision, where one's vision for near objects is better than for far.[15]
3) Tunnel vision: *Retinitis pigmentosa*—A condition in which the visual field is severely constricted so much that it results in the loss of peripheral vision. The loss of peripheral vision is the

inability to see the outer area of your field of vision, though you can still detect movement, shapes, and images.[16]

One more point, and I will bring this to a close. I promise.

This information can be summarized as unless one has 20/20 vision, if they have any other vision impairment as stated here, that person would be limited in what they would perceive as an image. The image they *see* would be out of focus either due to not being close enough or far enough or being outside their field of view, where they could capture the entire image if it wasn't centered enough.

In persons with impaired vision, eyesight would be severely limited, their brain's ability to conceive that image would potentially be gravely challenged, most likely resulting in it not being able to *see* a clear image at all. Your eyes have limited vision and, by default, *you* have been limited!

Ta-da, we made it through Visual Acuity 101. Good job!

I believe I have clearly defined our normal visual acuity aka eyesight.

Now, to conclude my point of mental sight aka our "mind's eye" in comparison to just normal eyesight, I must state my view of why the *imagination* is so much more the *requirement* for vision than one's eyesight alone.

Let's look at simple definition of our mental sight aka our mind's eye:[17]

1) the mental faculty of *conceiving imaginary* or recollected scenes;
2) the mental picture *so conceived.*

For all intents and purposes; reality = eyesight and imagination = mental sight aka our mind's eye.

## Reality and Imagination Flow in Opposite Directions

Christopher Wanjek, published, an article in *Live Science* 2014, called "Imagination and Reality Look Different in the Brain."[3b] This article reported a discovery was made by researchers who found that reality and imagination flow in different directions in the brain: "the visual information from real events that the *eyes see* flows 'up' from the brain's occipital lobe to the parietal lobe, but *imagined images* flow 'down' from the parietal to the occipital." Think of it as a mechanical highway, where absorbing reality and activating imagination use the same brain functions but just in the opposite flow.

These functions of the brain happen in the cerebrum. The functions of the cerebrum include: the senses of temperature, touch, vision, and hearing, the initiation of movement and coordination of movement as well as judgment, reasoning, problem-solving, emotions, and learning. More specifically, the right side of the cerebrum is medically known to control *creativity*, spatial ability, along with artistic and musical skills.

Though its implications are still unclear, this information may lead to a better understanding of how imagination is connected to memory and works in the brain. However, Christopher Bergland, on September 17, 2013 in *Psychology Today*, posted an article, "The "Right Brain" Is Not the Only Source of Creativity,"[18] this article reports the contrary. He shares that the researchers from Dartmouth College have shown this to be false: "human imagination *does not come **only** from the right hemisphere* of the cerebrum. Creativity and imagination require a *widespread neural network* in the brain." In fact, employing *imagination* involves eleven areas of the brain. Don't worry we won't be discussing those eleven areas at this time.

In a TEDx Mile High Talk, Kendra Sand, September 19, 2019, "Where Does Imagination Come From?"[3], had this to say about the imagination, "what is being reported here is, "through this intricate process, humans are able to consciously manipulate images, deconstruct symbols, come up with new ideas and theories, and . . . solve complex problems." All through the imagination!

This is important to know because if imagination came only from the right side of the brain, it, too, would be limited in imagery and vision for those who had been impaired by injuries to the right side of the brain. We've come to understand that there is no limit to the imagination and how the brain is able to manipulate images, deconstruct symbols, come up with new ideas and theories, and solve complex problems!

The imagination has *no* limits! To construct your vision, it is not dependent on what it sees through your eyesight but your mind's eye, where creativity is widespread *and* will construct for you an image as far as your imagination aka mental sight aka your mind's eye will take you.

You will never be limited in what you can see ever again. You're welcome!

Therefore, the statement I opened this chapter with I must reiterate:

*Vision —You must see something to create something,*
*and, if it doesn't exist, then you must imagine it.*
—Author's Quote

Wait, there is one other notation for those who have those investigative minds.

## *Aphantasia* and Memory

An article in *'verywell mind'-"An Overview of Aphantasia,"-written by Kendra Cherry* stated, that "recently, researchers have discovered a condition of unknown causes, the exact nature and its impact of which is not totally yet clear, known as aphantasia, (aphantasia is a lack of visual imagery, as *phantasia* is Greek for imagination).[19] This research also suggests that this condition may have a negative impact on memory. While little is known about aphantasia, one possible benefit of this lack of visual memory some might say is that people who have the condition could be less likely to be troubled by intrusive recollections or disturbing flashbacks."[20]

Okay, this would seemingly debunk my closing adamant statement, right? But I'm not done . . .

The clarification being, people with aphantasia *do* experience visual imagery *while dreaming*. This suggests that it is only intentional, voluntary visualization that is affected by this phenomenon. This is possible because what the brain does during wakefulness is different than what it does while dreaming. The imagery of dreams originates from the bottom-up processes controlled by the brainstem. This notation is contributed by the Neurologist Adam Zeman— as explained in the BBC's *Science Focus* 2018 magazine written by Jonas Schlatter of Berlin. Zeman estimates that aphantasia affects about 2 percent of the population.[21]

## Can You See God's Vision for You?

> Vision- You must *see* something to create something,
> and if it doesn't exist, then you must imagine it.

I needed to repeat my definition about vision here so that I can emphasize on how it is necessary for us to now see what God sees for us, through our imagination, from within us. We are already operating in an imagination mode when we create most anything anyway. I would suggest that we just have never stopped to visualize or evaluate it in that manner.

Take, for instance, a recipe. When we duplicate a recipe from scratch or pre-packaged ingredients, we create that recipe based on how we *imagine* it should be. Yes, of course, we may be able to see a picture of it and therefore attempt to duplicate it, *but* with or without the picture, that does not preclude our imagination guiding how we will create it.

Let's discuss this example: baking a chocolate cake. Take a recipe of simple cake ingredients like flour, milk, butter, eggs, salt, sugar of some type, and chocolate icing of choice, basic ingredients. There will be some who will *imagine* this cake to become a two-layer yellow cake with chocolate icing. Others, will imagine a chocolate cake with chocolate icing. Those with even more of an imagination will create a decadent chocolate cake with specialty chocolate icing, and those with even *greater* imaginations will see and create even more extravagant types of chocolate cakes, such as German chocolate, fudge chocolate, devil's food chocolate, chocolate mousse, Black Forest, gluten-free chocolate, chocolate torte, double chocolate, chocolate roll, sea salt chocolate, Kahlua chocolate, and raspberry chocolate cakes. Now, of course, it goes without saying that this is, by no means, an all-inclusive list of the variations of chocolate cakes that can be created, but I believe the point has been made.

Now, let's put all of this into context.

It must be understood that the *variations* of cakes that were created were based on each baker's imagination! The ingredients were the same, but based on what each saw with their imagination, they *added* to what they saw to create what they'd imagined. It wasn't just a mere attempt to duplicate a visualized picture, then perform a copy-and-paste function, imitating only what was externally seen, *au contraire*, baking the precise cake each baker imagined is a function of their creative ability cultivating what was externally seen, then expanding upon it internally within their mind's eye as they created it, producing originality every time, even if it's just a pinch of an ingredient different.

It is here that I must ask, can you see the *variations* of you—the you that God has already created within you that needs to be discovered by you and then distributed unto the world through *your* imagination, the imagination of you and how you see yourself using your gifts, talents, or sphere of influence to impact the world? (*See* chapter four: Where Do I Belong?)

May I offer a metaphor as a tool to measure your imagination level and create your vision?

Are you *farsighted*?

Farsightedness: where one's vision is better for distant objects than for near.

Has your imagination limited you to be able to see only things so far in the distance that you think that they are unobtainable? Perhaps it may have even become comfortable for you to know that they are so distant that you don't have to imagine them at all; you have already put them on the "will never happen for me" list. So, why even attempt it?

Have you found yourself saying, "this is going to take more effort and be too hard to do or to get, so why try?" Right? Wrong! Actually, it was just as much of an effort to go after the "easier" thing even though most likely that wasn't your vision for yourself at all, right?

Unfortunately, for many of us, what we don't factor in is that energy is energy, effort is effort, it's all the same. We just need to know how to apply to the right sources to maximize the benefit and reap the rewards thereof. Have you ever heard the expression, "Where the mind goes, the energy flows"? Well, it's true. Just as the adage "You can do whatever or become whatever you set your *mind* to" is true.

Okay, let's continue.

Are you *nearsighted*?

Principle 1—See It

Nearsightedness: where one's vision for near objects is better than for far.

Perhaps your imagination has led you to believe that this is your personal best. I suppose it can be considered better than farsightedness, but does it also have its disadvantages? Can nearsightedness be a bad thing? Yes, because it, too, has its limits.

One's imagination can't be viewed as acquiring or achieving something simply because what we desire is seemingly so close as to be considered within arm's reach. That's how most get bitten by snakes; you are too close! Imagination shouldn't be thought of as being corralled into a simple, small square footage of real estate of one's mental creativity simply because it appears to be within an easy reach that requires minimal effort. We have too many of those short-sighted imaginations amongst us. Let us take note, that those who imagine just barely enough, should consider if it's much of an imagination at all!

There is no challenge to this mindset, no true origination; in fact, it is almost done by memorization of something seen or previously done, and not by use of the imagination at all. And yes, there is a psychological difference between memorization and imagination.

I would like to propose an idea for agreement: let's consider that just because something is so close in proximity that it may only *appear* to be your best imagination of who you are and what your influence may be, when actually, it could be just capturing a snapshot of you in a moment in time!

Do you have *tunnel vision?*

Tunnel vision: in which the visual field is severely constricted, that peripheral vision is lost and you are unable to see the outer area of your field of vision.[22]

Our definition as it applies to the defectiveness of eyesight is clear; *WebMD* defines tunnel vision as 'peripheral vision loss' when, "you see everything in front of you, but everything above, below, and around you goes black. It's like you're looking through a narrow tube or a tunnel."[7c] And finally, the *Merriam-Webster Dictionary* defines it as: "an extreme narrowness of viewpoint: narrow-mindedness, also: single-minded concentration on one objective."[23]

We have now examined the medical and scholastic definitions. Now we must metaphorically look at it the idea of sight or vision and appreciate its relevancy.

Metaphorically, tunnel vision denotes the *reluctance* to consider alternatives to one's preferred line of thought, the tendency to *focus* exclusively on a single or limited goal or point of view.

Let's make the following comparisons of tunnel vision to our imagination and creativity in the manner to how we see ourselves. If one suffers from tunnel vision, then our imagination is severely reduced to only being able to see ourselves at the level or position we are currently on because we are either unable or *reluctant* to consider another view or image of ourselves other than what is only seen in front of us. Have you heard this saying while growing up as a child, typically said to us by our parents with a voice of harsh instruction, "Look where you are walking!" This was to imply we were walking and looking in two different directions. If we weren't careful, this often led to falls, accidents, slips, mistakes, or worst, tragedies. This caution should cause us to change our path so that we would walk where we are looking.

Interestingly enough, this is a great example of someone *not* having tunnel vision, so much so, they were able to detect something out of their peripheral view of enough significance it distracted them from where they were actually headed and caused them to turn. Now, of course, our parents thought they were teaching us rules of safety, and I would not disagree, but is it also possible that even then we were learning how to see not only what was in front of us but what is *around* us? And with great cultivation of our vision, we learn how to appreciate life and begin to see a world that is bigger than us. In the same way, we also learn to actually see *us* through our imagination and become bigger than who we currently think ourselves to be, and we realize that without us, the world would be missing an intricate part of the fabric of life that all must contribute to.

This should help us to understand how much we have to offer. It is through our imagination that we can identify our position in the world, where we can effectively give of our gifts, talents, and influence. How many areas of the world are lacking what we have to offer? Does it matter that your imagination seems so big that it appears impossible? No! Remember, in a world that is big, we need big imaginations, superlative ones!

I am confident that some of our greater things in life that we have been made aware of, come to appreciate, and had or currently use were all created by the imaginations of the "impossible thinkers."

Walt Disney—While living and working on a farm in the small town of Marceline, Missouri, as a boy, animals had a huge impact on his life. It was here that he began to draw animals and indulge his *imagination*. Mr. Disney's exposure to rural life influenced him throughout his career, and his passion and imagination grew from his fascination of drawing animals.[24] And as we know, the animals that he drew were not your typical farm animals: Pluto, Donald Duck, Oswald the Lucky Rabbit, Pete, Jiminy Cricket, King Louie, Horace Horsecollar, Ludwig Von Drake, Clarabelle Cow, Julius Cat, Baloo, and, of course, the iconic Mickey and Minnie Mouse. So where did those other animals come from?

I would suggest that he was able to see beyond what he saw, and by choosing not to be limited, his imagination allowed him to create what he did not yet see.

Mr. Walt Disney has contributed his gift and influence of his *greater self* to the world, and we now have the enjoyment of Disneyland and Disney World and so much more.

And we all know the rest, as they say . . . is history!

*All our dreams can come true, if we have the courage to pursue them.*
*It's kind of fun to do the impossible.*
*The way to get started is to quit talking and begin doing.*
*—Walt Disney*

Let's look at a few more persons who have had huge imaginations. We will note that they clearly did not have tunnel vision when it came to seeing themselves influencing life with their visions. These persons may not have been as well-known as Mr. Walt Disney, which is why I selected him first. I want us to see how well and how much we, too, can make an impact on the world. Regardless of whether or not the world speaks of it as often, it does not diminish the impact we can make. Remember, our vision of ourselves and our ability to imagine and create is not predicated on the accolades of men, but more so without us, the world would be missing an intricate part of the *fabric of life that* we all must contribute to.

Let me introduce to you three more people who have historically impacted the world in magnificent ways, but may not be as well known.

Shirley Ann Jackson—born on August 5, 1946, in Washington, DC. Her parents, Beatrice and George Jackson, strongly valued education and encouraged her in school. She graduated in 1964 as valedictorian from Roosevelt High School. While a student, she found time to do volunteer work at Boston City Hospital and tutored students at the Roxbury YMCA. After graduation, Miss Jackson also began classes at MIT that same year. She wrote her thesis on solid-state physics, a subject then in the forefront of theoretical physics. Miss Jackson became the first African-American woman to receive a doctorate from MIT. She has a BS in physics and a PhD in theoretical elementary particle physics, both from MIT.

Miss Jackson went on to invent the technology responsible for caller ID and call-waiting, the portable fax, and the fiber-optic cable. These all stem from the days at AT&T Bell Labs, where she conducted research in theoretical physics, solid state and quantum physics, and optical physics.[25]

I would have to submit that Miss Jackson was able to see more of what was missing than what was evident. Additionally, she had the ability to see herself as the one being able to bring her vision into existence. With her imagination, she did not allow herself to be limited; hence she saw beyond what was and created what wasn't.

Miss Shirley Jackson has contributed her gift and her influence *of her greater self* to the world, and we now have telecommunication space, including the touch-tone telephone, portable fax, caller ID, call-waiting, the fiber-optic cable, and so much more. And the advancement of this initial telecommunication technology has ultimately led to the plethora of communication technologies that we have today.

*Treasure your curiosity and nurture your imagination.*
*Have confidence in yourself. Do not let others put limits on you.*
*Dare to imagine the unimaginable.*
—Dr. Shirley Ann Jackson

Marie Van Brittan Brown—was a nurse and innovator from Queens, New York. Although she was a full-time nurse, she recognized the security threats to her home, was uneasy in her neighborhood, and felt the police were unreliable. So, she took matters into her own hands. Miss Brown *envisioned* a home security system and then *devised* a system that would alert her of strangers at her door and contact relevant authorities as quickly as possible. In 1966, she invented a video home security system along with her husband, Albert Brown, an electronics technician. In the same year, they applied for a patent for their innovative security system, which was granted in 1969.

Her original invention consisted of peepholes, a camera, monitors, and a two-way microphone. The finishing touch was an alarm button that, when pressed, would immediately contact the police. Her patent laid the groundwork for the modern closed-circuit television system that is widely used for surveillance, home security systems, push-button alarm triggers, crime prevention, and traffic monitoring. Miss Brown's device also led to the now nearly universal CCTV (closed circuit television) surveillance in public areas, aka Big Brother.[26] According to a

2016 *New Scientist* report, 100 million concealed closed-circuit cameras are now in operation worldwide.[27]

It is obvious that Miss Brown definitely saw more than what meets the eye. Not only did she see a need for more, but she also saw that her solution for that need should be able to be accessible from a multitude of locations and all at the same time. And she imagined that she was the one to do it! This becomes imagination at its best, truly going within one's self and removing all limits of a task as convoluted as this and taking the imagination to heights not yet explored.

Miss Brown felt neither hindered nor defeated by what wasn't. She was fueled by "fear" and empowered by her imagination of what could be; she created out of herself what should be!

Marie Van Brittan Brown has contributed her gift and her influence *of her greater self* to the world, and now, over fifty years later, Miss Brown's technology is installed in millions of homes and offices worldwide. Her contribution has allowed us to feel a little bit safer in our coming and going in everyday life.

> *She was fueled by "fear" and empowered*
> *by her imagination of what could be;*
> *she created out of herself what should be!*
> —*Author's Quote*

Malala Yousafzai (aka Malala)—at fifteen years old, a Taliban gunman shot her for going to school. After surviving this cowardly assassination attempt, the Pakistani activist turned this tragedy into a movement. She's devoted her life to fighting for female education across the map, earning her spot among the many historic servant leaders. Miss Malala saw herself not only as setting out to make a difference but willing to pay an ultimate sacrifice in doing so. Miss Malala saw past the reality of the constant threats to her life as she stood on the principles, she believed in. Miss Malala had a *vision* for a better educational opportunity for children, and this gave her the imagination that she could create that. During a BBC interview conducted on March 13, 2017, Malala stated her "goal is to make sure every child, a girl and a boy, they get the opportunity to go to school."

On her eighteenth birthday, the educational activist opened up a secondary school in Lebanon for Syrian refugee girls!

What makes Malala a compassionate leader is her ability to translate her own experiences and connect with global citizens facing other adversities. Part of being a servant leader is finding that intrinsic motivation to help others.[28]

I submit, Miss Malala was nearly denied the ability to try to make a difference, but she recognized that it was more important to make the difference, even if she was to lose her life in doing so. You see, once you see yourself outside of yourself, and your imagination shows you the real you, you've discovered your creative ability, and there is no denying what you can do; there is nothing left but to do it now! In her imagination, she has already canceled fear as a factor; therefore, everything else becomes a win-win, even in adversity.

Malala Yousafzai (aka Malala) has contributed her gift and influence *of her greater self,* and at the age of eighteen, she was a very young educational activist, who has since opened up a secondary school in Lebanon for Syrian refugee girls. Her contribution has privileged her with a Nobel Peace Prize in 2014. At age seventeen, she became the youngest person to receive this prize.

*The servant leader is servant first. . . It begins with the natural feeling that one wants to serve, to serve first.
Then conscious choice brings one to aspire to lead.*
—Malala Yousafzai (aka Malala)

**Learning How to Pivot**

I must point out that in all of these great notable contributions, each person demonstrated the ability to pivot. They saw and operated in life such as it was, but they had a disdain for what they saw because they did not have tunnel vision and did not experience the lack of ability to notice what was happening around them versus what was only in front of them. Additionally, they did not limit this view to seeing themselves as having only one focus straight ahead.

Great imaginations have to pivot from what you only see in front of you to what you see around you to what you must create from the imagination within you.

What did these influential people have in common? What was the entry point of their pivot? They had the capability to recognize that what they currently did or were doing (more commonly known as our livelihoods) was not the only thing they were meant to do. Subsequently, they tapped into themselves, imagined the area of lack in the world that they could submit their gift, talent, or use their sphere of influence, and created the solution. They had no preplanning or formal preparation. What they did have was an unlimited imagination that relayed a problem to their *greater self,* and what they saw, they created! Hence, they each improved an area of life with great abilities beyond their everyday existence by merely seeing with their mind's eye.

They pivoted!

*We must all remember that winning is not only about finishing but more so about starting!*
—Author's Quote

As I bring this to a close, I must introduce one other type of vision merely for definition, application, and conclusion.

*Panoramic Sight*

Panoramic Vision, View: showing a full or wide view, all-inclusive, fully embracing, global, exhaustive, no limit on distance view.

It is here that I will make the case that unequivocally, the best "eyesight" of all is when one has the capacity for panoramic vision when you can see all things from all perspectives, without limitation, for the greater good, yet with mental accountability and moral judgment. Panoramic vision and the imagination can be considered synonymous. However, let me be explicitly clear that my expression of panoramic view and its synonymous relationship to our imagination is when we view life through the lens of God.

God's view of us in the world is without limits of what is or what shall be because with God's lens, everything already *is*. Our contributions become the manifestation of it. God's lens is without any biases or judgment to any one area of deficiency *over* another in life. It is for the greater good of mankind without prejudices toward any particular person, place, or thing. His lens encompasses the vastness of the world, while He has given us the capacity to repair, restore, resurrect, retain, refurbish, replace, and recreate.

If we can have a panoramic view with the ability to pivot from what we do to what we can create, then I would suggest that we have the true ability to see with our mind's eye and contribute *our greater self* to the world as we imagine it to be, not as it is!

*There are no limits to the imagination of the mind's eye; it cannot be considered impaired or defective, unlike typical eyesight.*
—Author's Quote

As you evaluate yourself to identify if you have the ability to imagine and create, ask yourself these questions as you view them through your mind's eye:

- *Where* do you see it? (person, place, or thing)
- *When* did you see it? (person, place, or thing)
- *How* do you imagine yourself contributing or creating it? (person, place, or thing)
- *Who* do you see? (person, place, or thing)
- *What* do you see? (person, place, or thing)

Epitome of imagination—what the mind can *conceive*, it can *achieve!*

# Seven

## *Principle 2—Write It . . . Engrave It Plainly on Clay Tablets*
## *—Habakkuk 2:2 AMP*

---

Writing reinforces what we see because everything we see begins with a thought, and the thought evolves as we write. Why write, one might ask? While there are many reasons as to why we should, one reason is simply this: it would be a fatal mistake to think that once you have imagined *your greater self*, that without writing out what you saw, you would retain the details of it. Some might say, "I have a photographic memory; I remember everything," and we all probably have heard someone say that at some time. But the truth of the matter is our photographic memories, such as they are, are snapshots of a moment in time that only last for a brief period of time. This is actually known as "eidetic memory."[29] An eidetic memory is the ability to see an object soon after you look away. For most people, the image lasts mere seconds or less than one second.

To get an idea of how well your brain makes use of eidetic memory, look at an object and close your eyes, and see how long you can still see the object in your mind's eye. Can you see it? Everyone has use of eidetic memory to a degree.

An article written in *Better Help,* dated December 31, 2020, reported that few people truly have a photographic memory. Even people with a photographic memory may not retain these memories for a long period. Most photographic memories only last a few months at most, as they are not relayed to long-term memory. With a photographic memory, the eidetic memory is transferred to the short-term memory for storage, allowing it to be recalled much later. However, while most people make some limited use of eidetic memory, photographic memory is rarer. This is why it is much more reliable to write things down as opposed to trying to remember what you saw in detail merely by recalling photo memory only.

Writing leaves an imprint in our minds of what we have visualized. It gives us the reference points of what we have seen. Then, line by line, it allows us to create our vision. Once we create it in our minds, writing it helps us to become it.

Let's be reminded for the purpose of this book that you are writing about what you see for your life. We are *exploring, expressing,* and *explaining* our greater self to not only ourselves but to others. Let's discuss these three simple writing values in detail.

**Exploring**. Some of you have never stopped to imagine yourself outside of your daily livelihood or the perfunctory duties that we do on a daily basis. It has been said, "What you see is what you get!" and for some, this may be true. But *here*, we are discovering that our lives have much greater meaning than what meets the eye, which is why we have learned to shift the view to our mind's eye view. This is learning how to go within and see and discover our many gifts, talents, and sphere of influence that we will contribute to the world. When doing so, you may not readily see your greater self and what you have to offer. It will become essential to write down in detail what you do see. Date it, and some may *even* find it is necessary to add the time of day and place. Why? Because our environment and activities contribute to our thoughts.

For example, perhaps you see yourself speaking to a group of youths for encouragement about getting an education, helping them to achieve a better life, to reach goals earlier in life, and accomplish career paths of their interest. But your environment may currently have a temporary negative atmosphere about school, poor educational programs, bad school districts, job losses, a failing economy, and graduates who have not been able to obtain careers of their choice. Subliminally, this could then persuade you that what you imagined for your greater self is not a worthwhile contribution to explore or even consider writing down. You may decide, "I need to try to imagine myself doing something else." You may decide that the whole idea of even thinking of trying to persuade youth about getting an education in the world of technology, where you can google almost anything that you may want to know, that education may almost be a misnomer.

Once you have this vision of yourself and decide to entertain some of these thoughts, you will need to do the following: regardless of whichever negative reason tries to impact your thought at that time, you would want to write it down, date it, and note the environment and place. This will help you realize that when this imagination of your greater self and your contribution to the world continues to revisit you in your mind's eye, and you see yourself making an impact, small, big, or otherwise, it doesn't change who *you* were created to be and the lives you were meant to impact with your life. Nor will it change what your contribution is. In fact, it will most likely solidify who your greater self is. Therefore, your initial negative thoughts should not be granted the final say in your life and persuade you otherwise.

I want to convey a fact so that you will not discount the image of your greater self, based only on thoughts about yourself. Many of the images we have about ourselves are associated with our thoughts or the thoughts of others. Additionally, many of our thoughts are influenced by our environment. Because our environment can often change for a number of reasons, our thoughts about ourselves can be like the changing colors of a chameleon. Meaning, our thoughts at any one point in time would be unreliable as an *absolute* source of certainty as to who we are.

Allow me to quantify this forementioned statement with the following excerpt. Author Ben Hardy, noted that in 2005 the *National Science Foundation* published an article summarizing research on human thoughts per day. "It was found that the average person has about 12,000 to 60,000 thoughts per day. Of those thousands of thoughts, 80 percent were negative, and 95 percent were exactly the same repetitive *negative* thoughts as the day before."[30]

We can see that one of the tendencies of the mind is to focus on the negative and play the same *sad* songs over and over again. This study was followed by the following; *Professor Robert Leahy of Cornell University in 2005*, reported scientists found that, "firstly, 85 percent of what we worry about never happens. Secondly, with the 15 percent of the worries that did happen, 79 percent of the subjects discovered that either they could handle the difficulty better than expected or that the difficulty taught them a lesson worth learning. The conclusion is that 97 percent of our worries are baseless and result from an unfounded pessimistic perception."

That information is worth knowing as you write for the reason that if you have a negative thought about who you are or what you will do, you must keep writing what you see about yourself anyway. If you are having a bad day, this information will change from time to time. And if the day you are writing is a good day, your image of you should be in alignment with your thoughts. Remember, you are exploring you. Don't stop until all of your greater self has revealed itself. Writing will preserve this imagination as an idea and a lasting memory.

*The more you write, the more your writing will convey your thoughts of what you see, who you are, and what you have to contribute.*
—*Author's Quote*

*Principle 2—Write It . . .Engrave It Plainly on Clay Tablets*

**Expressing.** Writing is an invaluable tool to have when you are discovering your life's purpose. Not only does it allow you to explore you, but it also gives you the opportunity to express you.

People often say, "I'm just expressing who I am." This sometimes equates to very unique and fashionable styles of dress, hairstyles, hair colors, styles of living, modes of transportation, perhaps what people choose to eat, where they go, what they say, what they believe, and, yes . . . who they believe themselves to be! Yes, the human race is unique in so many areas, *yet* we are really very much alike. Hmmm.

Who do you express yourself to be? I mean, once you have an image of yourself and know to really be productive in that image or make your contribution to the world with your image, how will you express you, by writing? No, I'm not suggesting you should become a writer; however, as you might guess, I am partial to writers. Nonetheless, you will be writing out your image of yourself, again, as seen in your mind's eye, through expressive writing. What is expressive writing? I'm glad you asked!

John F Evans Ed.D, *Psychology Today,* in an article dated August 15, 2012, had this to say about expressive writing: "Expressive writing is a cornerstone of wellness and writing connections. If you are not familiar with it, you may be asking: 'Just what is expressive writing, and how is that related to my wellness?'"[31]

Expressive writing comes from our core. It is personal and emotional writing without regard to form or other conventions like spelling, punctuation, and verb agreement. It simply expresses what is on your mind and in your heart.

Expressive writing pays more attention to *feelings* than the events, memories, objects, or people in the contents of the narrative. Expressive writing is not so much what happened as it is how you feel about what happened or is happening.

My personal belief is that expressive writing also allows you to create what you would like to see happen and how you would like to feel. Remember, the beauty of what you are doing is writing creatively about what you see that has not yet happened but hope to. You control the outcome of this by writing about how you currently *feel* about what you see and how you *hope to feel* or *want to feel* about what you see.

As the author of your greater self, you get to construct your own outcome. You are not waiting for you to get to where you see yourself; you are writing what is supposed to take place and how it should take place. In effect, you're scheduling your feelings, emotions, and outcome ahead of time simply by investing enough into your greater self to write it out. You shift a potential negative outcome that is often formulated out of lack of planning and contributed to by lack of writing into a positive, purposeful outcome because your actions produced a paradigm shift.

It might serve you well to understand that expressive writing may make some people briefly feel a bit saddened or down after expressive writing—especially on the first day or so, but usually these feelings will go away in an hour or two. Why saddened? Because you are seeing you with your mind's eye, discovering the greater you—your core value—all that your life's purpose has to really offer. These discoveries may cause us to discover some of the hindrances to why we are so delayed in becoming or identifying our greater selves. We may discover deliberate attempts of those who try to induce harmful schemes to prevent us from ever evolving. Also, we may be overwhelmed with anxiety as to how we will become what we see. Or it could be a myriad of many other things, but these saddened emotions will pass.

The best thing that you can ever do for yourself is to identify your feelings, evaluate them for what they are, respond to them in the best positive way that you can for your best health, and then keep it moving. Writing expresses *who you are to you* first and to others second. Once the introductions have been made, you must evolve into your greater self. Your life has a purpose!

*Writing expresses who you are to you first and to others second.*
*—Author's Quote*

**Explaining.** When we are writing about ourselves, we are really making an effort to explain ourselves. No one may have asked any questions, but it's like having a FAQ list and answering the most frequently asked questions ahead of time. Additionally, it allows us to take the opportunity to refine our ideas to others and ourselves.

The rule to offering explanations is to not over explain. People often like to give as many details about our lives as we can, like what we do, who told us to do it, how did you know to do it, and why did you decide to do it (this could be close friends, family, or associates asking this question). Heck, you might often find you didn't know you could do some things until you discovered it and did it! You will need to know that though people may ask, not everyone is privy to all the answers. Being asked and being obliged to answer are two very distinctively different things. Some people like information for two reasons only. Here, I will give you two guesses as to what that might be . . . okay, I'll tell you: gathering and gossiping! I think that's enough said. Let's keep going.

What are we really stating when we talk about explaining? We mean making what you have imagined in your mind's eye as clear as possible—not necessarily to anyone in particular—but to you. You will want to try to understand what you are seeing yourself contribute and then try to describe it. Some things you might imagine doing may have never been seen or done before, but don't be alarmed. In fact, that should become fascinating to you. You get to become something you don't have a blueprint for. You can detail it, describe it, and create it as best as you understand it. Your language to articulate it may be limited, but who cares? No one can tell you it's wrong; they most likely have never seen it before either. Should they declare that they have, kindly let them know, "Well, you haven't seen this one before. I haven't created it yet." Let that excite you.

Be free with your description of what you see, and don't be afraid of what you see; therefore, don't attempt to downplay it because it may seem larger than you, or as some would say . . . larger than life. This is your *greater self;* it should be larger than you. It can't be only as big as your life, then you will be contributing only what you think you can produce. The *greater you* have not yet been tapped into or discovered. You are clarifying you as you write it. And you will clarify it again as you write more, edit, rewrite it, and, of course, as you revisit the imagination you have for it. It is your contribution of your gift to the earth, not a replica of someone else's, even if it appears to be similar. Remember, if you haven't don't it yet, it hasn't been seen yet by anyone, not even you. You must imagine it, write it, and create it!

I implore you that you must write your vision down. Not writing it down has the propensity to *alter* the desired outcome of anything we hope to accomplish or have envisioned, big or small. It's the difference between something that has great significance as a contribution to someone, person, place, or thing and it being accomplished or never seeing the light of day. Its existence remains only a thought, vision, or imagination! Your life is unmistakably full of purpose and significance, destiny, fortitude, and greatness. It is designed to impact another, even if you never thought so. Can you believe in yourself enough to know that your life is worth the investment of writing down at least the description of what you have imagined? I've heard it said, "Some things you should just take to your grave," and that may be true, but don't let it be your life's purpose! Don't bury it. Fulfill it! Write it down!

*Remember, if you haven't don't it yet, it hasn't been seen yet by anyone, not even you. You must imagine it, write it and create it!*
*—Author's Quote*

As you reflect on the concept that writing is a necessity to conveying our thoughts and clarifying what we see, let's put this into a personal perspective. Challenge yourself to begin writing here. Take a little practice by answering or elaborating on these statements. You will immediately notice how writing things down can help you organize your thoughts and ideas.

**How Writing Things Down Organize Your Thoughts and Help Develop Your Purpose**

1) Writing allows you to declutter your mind of potential self-sabotaging thoughts about your vision. You are organizing your thoughts for clarity of *(write your vision here)*
2) Organizing your thoughts is a way of processing your emotions and connecting them to *(write your vision here)*
3) Once you have written your vision, write it again. This time leave out the doubts noted in the first draft. Then write it again, leaving out the second-guessing of doubts removed in the second draft and was most likely added back in, then… yes, write it again. Realizing '*perfect practice makes perfect*' (see next chapter)
4) Writing your vision out a series of time produces an agreement with your mind's eye and your thoughts to produce it
5) Written organized thoughts helps your vision to grow from what you see to what you now can imagine becoming
6) Written organized thoughts makes you commit to *(write your vision here)*

# Eight

# *Principle 3—Read It, Run with It*

*"the one who reads it will run . . .
it hurries toward the goal."
—Habakkuk 2:2–3 AMP*

---

Read what you have now written daily so that you may begin to run with it.

Now, let's begin putting everything into practice. I have dubbed this next principle *the* most significant one of all. It is essential to begin reading, learning, applying, researching, studying, and then running with it . . . quickly! Running with what you have seen, written, and becoming to understand is your greater self and your contribution to the world.

If I can give an analogy for clarity, it would be this, "reading and running with it" is like having a cooking recipe of a succulent meal, requiring a huge pot of many fine ingredients for this exquisite fine dining meal that all are waiting for, but the cook is not doing anything with them. So, everybody is just waiting, even you! These ingredients, with no next step to get them into becoming a fine meal, are a meal in theory only. So, someone created it, wrote it down, and may have even read it over, but they never ran with it or put it into action. This may be a great recipe, but it is useless to anyone who is supposed to benefit from it, especially the one who created it. The question then would lead someone to ask, "Is it really a recipe?"

The word *running* as an adjective implies movement or action, such as fly . . . flying, sing . . . singing, cook . . . cooking, read . . . reading, and run . . . running! You must take action to begin bringing it together for full evolvement to take place. Don't wait.

Reading and running with a vision should jump-start an action plan of putting into practice what you envision. The practicing of it is just a process or step to evaluate what you have as your plan. You must begin practicing what you wrote down.

We have all heard "practice makes perfect," right? This may be the common colloquial; however, I prefer that statement in this manner: "perfect practice makes perfect." Do you hear the difference? Well, let's put it to the test. The process is the actual, *ongoing* activity of reviewing the operations, reading the duties, discussing the functions, and relaying the execution of a command and, most importantly, the discipline to carry it out to completion. Only then can you say you are *running* with it.

Have you ever noticed how some people have great plans, and they can even show you what it looks like on paper, even in every exhausting detail! Then three months, six months to a year or more, when you see them again, they haven't done anything with it. And it's not like it wasn't a good plan with great desirable outcomes, meticulous planning phases, or seemingly flawless steps to acquiring it, *but* they had not made the personal commitment to dedicate themselves to a process and work it. They did not have a perfect practice, which makes it perfect! They didn't even implement a practice of any type.

They were the chief of operations, the president of the company, the person who can make it happen or stop it from happening. All the decisions started and stopped with them, and since they failed to run with it, indeed, it stopped with them.

## Principle 3—Read It, Run with It

Is it possible that the decisions for your greater self to show up in your life never happened because after you had the vision for yourself and the ability to write it out, you then ran out of steam to carry it out? I hope not, but it certainly is possible.

Let's take this apart. A process, or running with it (we will use these two phrases interchangeably), must have a methodical approach. It must have a deliberate purpose with end results in mind, even after the first effort has been applied. Each effort should produce a result of some type. These results are not meant to be big results, just *any* result. Results bring a sense of accomplishment. Accomplishments bring a sense of achievement. Achievements bring a sense of completion. Completions brings a sense of confidence. Confidence brings a sense of courage. Courage brings a sense of resolution and a commitment to further accomplishments.

This process of running with it with an end result in mind creates a snowball effect of momentum that yields an expectation of complete fulfillment. These efforts in themselves become self-rewarding, which becomes its own inspiration. And though each next level of achievement typically will lead to a new challenge, the next new effort becomes the emotional equivalent of an adrenalin rush that will fuel the further efforts required.

Have you ever seen a fisherman fish? I'm sure many have said yes. I have too. Now, of course, just for the sake of clarification, I'm not a fisherman and am not necessarily interested in becoming one, but I have been out on a fishermen's pier on several occasions. Even fishermen need cheerleaders.

Let's continue. I have watched fishermen cast a fishing line with such great effort; the sound of the line unwinding and then landing that hook in the water sounds like a precision of great expertise, but it makes a mere "plop" sound in the water when it hits. It seemingly is not very impressive based on sound—not like an anchor being dropped over the side of a boat with a splash—it's just a soft "plop."

But I have come to understand that there is a method to the whole effort of casting a fishing line. First, the fishing line doesn't just have a hook on it; it may have a bobber with a hook for fishing in more shallow water, or it may have a sinker for keeping the hook in deeper water. Then, there are several types of bait, all specifically chosen with the intent of drawing the type of fish they hope to catch. Then, there are specific times of when to fish, decisions about where to fish, and choices about what type of water to fish in. Did I mention that there are even different types of fishing lines and fishing poles! Are you following me? Each decision is a deliberate effort for the purpose of accomplishing a specific result, catching a certain type of fish.

The method is purposeful, and a result is expected, even though the sound, to some, may not sound like much of an effort at all. Thus, it becomes incredible to see when they reel in these amazing large or small size gilled creatures for either game or dinner (I'm just saying) with seemingly the mere efforts they made. But those seemingly small efforts yielded an incredible result, sometimes so huge or small that they are surprised and excited either way. Why? Because a favorable result of any type is momentum in the right direction.

So, what do they do next? They reel that fish in with such skill of pulling and winding, pulling and winding, repeating the exact same effort bringing the *hooked* fish closer and closer to being the *caught* fish. They do this with care to not lose what they have worked so hard and patiently for. Then, they do something I thought certainly deserved mention—and can easily be considered an epitome of a methodical process that yields personal results—they unhook the fish very carefully and, depending on the size of the fish, they either keep it or throw it back. Then, they repeat those same steps over again, sometimes with just a slightly different effort, *but* their expectation of yielding *better* results is extraordinarily high.

The mere fact of them catching anything at all yields such a sense of accomplishment they become even more eager to reproduce that same amount of energy to hopefully gain *better* results when each of these carefully executed steps is repeated. They realize that the *additional* effort they exerted, even if appeared to be unchanged to the untrained person, was significant enough. They know they did something different, and they expect not only a different result but a better result. Wow! The effort and what it potentially yields becomes its own source of momentum, becoming its own inspiration.

In fact, each new next effort is never really the same because it is challenged by the next desired results, which is always to outdo what you did the first time! Goal achievements and accomplishments can produce an overwhelming emotion of success. These results should help us to understand that it is healthy and normal to always seek out the next challenge in our process of running with it, always with an expectation to conquering it. In other words, you become your own competition.

Now, for those of you who are *very* competitive (myself included), I believe you would agree with me that we are always looking for our "next personal best." But then, we must consider what happens each time we attempt to repeat *exerted energy* with an expectation to yield *maximum results*; our minds may be willing, but our body's physical ability most likely will become diminished or less energetic with each new effort. Expect it, and be okay with that!

**Producing Energy**

Producing the energy to work a process that has many pieces and requires a goal for each one will require a certain amount of energy and effort every time, and since physical energy slows, it must be generated on a repeated basis in the mind! The *mind* will have to demand the body to give 100-percent effort! So, how does one do that? You must go back to the last achievement and *build* on it as opposed to trying to *beat* it! The energy becomes different. Let me explain. Building on one's last achievement is producing one's own momentum. The momentum then creates motivation. Motivation creates opportunity, and opportunity produces results.

Think of momentum as a force unwilling to come to a halt. In sports, we often talk of a team having momentum to refer to a team on a winning streak that is *seemingly* unstoppable. And if they can think of themselves as unstoppable, they will produce an energy of being unstoppable. They may become fatigued in every effort they exert, but in their minds, they are unstoppable. This energy can be sensed by their opponent, and if they can convince their opponent they are unstoppable—guess what—they will *become* unstoppable.

Remember, in this scenario, you are your own competition. You will produce your own energy in your mind, creating your own momentum, creating your own motivation, becoming your own message, *becoming* unstoppable!

Here are two examples of potential energy. A drawn bow and a compressed spring both have potential energy. This is elastic potential energy, which results from stretching or compressing an object. For elastic materials, increasing the amount of stretch raises the amount of stored energy. Springs have energy when stretched or compressed. This example applies to the mind in its attempt to restart and re-energize the body. This is what needs to happen. The accomplishment from the last effort becomes the compressed spring for the physical energy that is needed when the body is preparing to exert itself for the next accomplishment and for whatever the next challenge may be. Many have called this "mind over matter" or "Where the *mind* goes, *energy* flows." And the best way to send energy to a part of the body that is already decreased in strength due to its last effort is that you don't want to tell yourself, "Okay, let's beat that." Instead, tell yourself, "Let's *repeat* that! Let's build on that!" Why? Because it's easier! It's always easier to merely repeat something that already works as opposed to trying to re-create something new each time, which is what this would be if you were trying to compete with yourself and beat your last effort. Each effort is new in and of itself; when it's been accomplished, you already have beaten the last effort!

Let life's experiences be your springboard to the next accomplishment!

> *You don't want to tell yourself okay, let's beat that,*
> *instead tell yourself, let's repeat that!*
> *—Author's Quote*

Reading and running with a vision should jump-start an action plan of putting into practice what you envision. I have given you another small challenge here. Use this small practice exercise to build your own steam for your contribution to life. Utilize this tool as if you were working your own business. Your life is your business.

**Five Ways to Create Momentum in Business: by Benard Mokua[32]**

1) Create a game plan and remain committed;
2) Set SMART goals:
    a. S—Specific (goals that are clearly defined)
    b. M—Measurable (goals whose progress can be measured)
    c. A—Attainable (goals that are possible to attain)
    d. R—Relevant (goals that are aligned to your vision)
    e. T—Time-based goals that have a definite period in which they should be attained;
3) Suspend your disbeliefs; develop a positive mindset;
4) Focus with intensity; and
5) Reward yourself for your achievements, especially the small ones.

# Nine

# *Principle 4—Wait for It . . .*

## *"though it delays, wait (patiently) for it."*
## *—Habakkuk 2:3 AMP*

---

**Timing Is Essential**

Don't let delays discourage you. While you wait, you need to be doing something; stay productive. Being actively and consistently productive will cause you to continuously produce quality outcomes. It will be the proof that the process works; it will yield results, reveal the benefits, and show forth the profits that are expected, and you will confidently exceed. No one sets out to work on something so diligently to produce something mediocre. It is understood that a productive person's genuine *effort* will lead to a successful *product*. Now, the product may need to be tested for maximum benefit of use, but you do have a product! And often you may have to wait to see the finished product fully evolve, but don't dismay!

We may not always see our efforts producing a product; we are just being productive for the task at hand. We are trying to ensure that there really is a means to the end. No one has time to waste! Time doesn't belong to us. And that is precisely why we shouldn't waste time. We have to position ourselves to be good stewards of time. We don't get time back!

I am a fan of one of many significant quotes out of the Good News Bible that says, *be mindful of your time, learn to count your days, be aware of them and apply wisdom and your heart to each day* (Ps. 90:12, author's paraphrase). Make each day count! Be productive! Don't just get up and have nothing planned. What did you have in mind for these brand new twenty-four hours of your life? Remember, this is not just a mediocre twenty-four hours of a day; this day is deliberate, intended, purposeful, and targeted for you to receive another twenty-four hours of the world's time!

This timeframe had you in mind, even if *you* didn't have you in mind. Let me say it this way, you have been given a gift, twenty-four hours, to accomplish something in your life! I implore you to not take that lightly. There are many who would love to have another twenty-four hours here on earth. In fact, if I took a small poll right now, each of you would be able to name one person, if not several. Be productive—produce something, anything—while you have the time available to you.

Now, that may seem like a paradox statement. Afterall, I said wait, now I'm saying to be productive. Let me give an illustration for clarity. A pregnant woman is expected to stay as active and productive as possible until she delivers, why? It helps her maintain stamina, strength, endurance, physical fitness and overall good health. Why is that necessary? Because she is positioning herself to produce the healthiest, "picture-perfect" version of her newborn she can. So, while she *waits* to deliver, (her healthy *envisioned* newborn), she *continues* valuable productivity to bring it into fruition. It's an oxymoron at best!

Let's continue.

Okay, let's address those who just said, "Produce what?" followed by "I don't know where to start," followed by "I can't," followed by "I don't have time," followed by, "I'm too busy" (which is different from "I don't *have* time;" you have time, just not for this). And there are countless other thoughts and reasons why some feel they just can't use their time productively. If you found yourself in agreement with any of these excuses, you are the ones who, most importantly, need to pay close attention to the following.

People who embrace this idea, who have convinced themselves to believe that they don't know what to produce or what to do with their gift of twenty-four hours are the same type of people who will ask others, "How did you do that?" or "When did you have time to do that?" or "I didn't know you could do that," followed by, "So, you know how to do that?" But all the productive people did that I am urging each of you to do is they didn't *squander* their time with meaningless self-limiting conversations designed to convince themselves by declaring, "I can't do it" or "I don't know how to."

Productive people simply took an extra minute to evaluate what they have envisioned, looked at what they wrote, and decided, "I will start *here*," meaning they began running with it or began the process with what they had so far, and they've pursued their idea until that which they have envisioned, which is huge, began to take place.

It is an unfortunate truth that many people are more interested in *admiring* other people's lives than creating and *living* their own. They have convinced themselves that their lives are less important and less exciting and less meaningful. They may have not realized that was what they were saying, but that is exactly what they have told themselves, perhaps not in so many words but by their inaction, and we all know actions speak later than words. And while they have taken the position to silently high-five someone else's life, they have silently discounted their own! How did they do that? By wasting time embarking on what they see. Whenever you are *unhurried* in taking steps or making moves on what you see as your life's purpose, *you* are the delay! Let's explore this a bit more.

Imagine you've conducted a series of interviews with some of your favorite Hollywood stars, celebrity greats, entertainers, performing artists, athletic superheroes, prestigious career builders, and renown-authors. Okay, we're done! We could name more, but I think you've got the idea. In these interviews, we discover amazing fun facts about these public personalities, like their living style, their start in life, their next great big thing . . . yada, yada, yada.

We engage ourselves culturally through mass media into the lives of these figures with countless hours of eye gazing, event catching, show watching, news gossiping, and reality show binging. Let's bear in mind that these many hours of life we've spent watching others we have literally given away because there is no return on our investment of time spent in mindless television watching! Sorry, that part of your life you don't get back. As we watch their lives in amazement, we wonder, "Why can't I do that?" Really? Can't do what, have an exciting, amazing life? Why can't you?

Here is my question to you: "What is it that you admired most about the lives of these people? Is it what their lives look like to you? What their lives seemingly represent, "the *good* life," a life of easy living? Do you admire these strangers so much that you have to live vicariously through their lives to gain a sense of appreciation of yours?" Ask yourself and be honest.

If so, then you must understand that what you don't see is the many years of effort behind the scenes that has now "produced" the end "product" that you do see! Their lives are a product of the same twenty-four hours that you have each day, but they have capitalized on those hours by maximizing their efforts of every hour given unto them! The difference should be apparent: they have placed a priority on their twenty-four hours that was "gifted" to them each day. They honored each day by inserting themselves into their day and producing something. And now what we see are lives we admire, talents we appreciate, and some things we even quietly resent. When all they did is they produced a product with their lives by treating their twenty-four hours each day as a gift to be valued and spent wisely. Yet, we continue to be participants in their lives and spectators in our own.

I strongly suggest that we must stop giving away parts of our lives in thirty minutes to an hour a show at a time. Let's begin producing our own lives. Can we start with where we are? No more delays!

**Start Where You Are**

Most people believe that some people are born talented, gifted, or are child prodigies. Though there may be some truth to that, I believe we *all* are gifted in some respect. I believe that there are those who take more time being *invested into* or *investing in* themselves early in life and begin cultivating the gifts they have discovered within them.

Why do I believe that? I am so glad you asked! Let's take a look at the following statement,

"We all have gifts. They differ according to the grace God has given to each of us" (Rom. 12:6 NIRV).

Some of you are probably saying, "Well, I already have a job." Some of you may have two or three jobs, and that's okay. In fact, simply stated a *job* is, "a regular remunerative position of employment." And yes, you must earn money to coexist in life with others. We have to be financially responsible to our obligations. And this could be one prime reason why some have appeared to not have produced anything as of yet, other commitments of their time! It is a fairly decent statement but not an all-inclusive reason. Here is why.

Allow me to ask the obvious question, "Have you reduced your life to identifying yourself with just a position of employment?" A mere job of any type, whether it's working for yourself or someone else, is that all your twenty-four hours are good for? If we are all just working and calling the segments of hours each day where we get paid, a job, we are missing a big insight into our lives. But we'll arrive there in a moment; stay with me.

If some of these jobs we have are seemingly nuisances, then why do we *admire* others who also have jobs? Why do we feel good about theirs and not about our own? I mean, you do realize all of those lives previously mentioned we admire and sacrifice hours from our lives to watch, they most likely will never come to appreciate, acknowledge, be grateful for, or ever know we even existed, and therefore they will never be able to say thank you. What they are doing that we admire so much is a *job*! Really! Uh, oh, did some of you just say ouch? It's okay, you'll feel better in a minute.

I must ask, why do we give so much more credence to what they are doing than we give our own lives and what we are doing? I'll tell you why. We are admiring what their lives have produced! We love the products of their lives! We don't see it as a job, only as something to *admire*. Let's pause right there for a moment.

Don't you see, we have not taken into consideration the committed efforts and daily contribution these personalities and entertainers have put into producing the product of their lives that we have admired. The interview we imagined would show us the long hours, failed attempts, pain, hard work, the naysayers, their own moments of self-defeat, the times when they decided they would just walk away, and those who did and then came back, or those who had the thought but decided it was better to just see it through. In other words, their careers became more than just a job. They wanted to *produce* something with their lives, and they *did*!

When you set out to produce something, you have to examine your life and see the value in it and experiment with ideas, thoughts, and make the required efforts to not just be aimlessly productive but to realize you are creating a product with your life, something of your passion, that brings you pleasure, that you can share with the world. Remove the focus of making money, not that you shouldn't seek to make money, but seek to produce something with your life. Seek to make an impact! Don't minimize your life with admiring someone else's life as if theirs is something more than yours because it isn't! They just decided to produce something with theirs and not just spend their time admiring others.

How big does your *something* have to be? It only needs to be as big as your heart can hold, mind can imagine, eyes can envision, and as much as your core values will guide you that will allow you to stay true to you!

**Producing the Gift**

How does one determine this product? Is it based on the job only? I thought that in this book, we are discovering that our life's purpose is not one-dimensional and not based solely upon our external environment of work and similar associations? But rather, our life's purpose should reflect our mind's eye vision and what we imagine ourselves doing that at the core of us, which houses our talents, gifts, contributions, and power of influence, was the thing that gave others the greatest reward and us the greatest pleasure. And yes, that is a fact. This is the quintessential existence of who we are, harboring that which we are supposed to contribute!

But, the exploration of the gift, the evolution of itself, the revealing of our power of influence, and our contribution to others doesn't just show up in our lives one day like a wandering lost pet looking for its owner.

It shows up in our lives as we become the wandering lost soul looking for our best self within ourselves.

It shows up as we begin longing for ourselves to meticulously start the cultivation process to becoming the contributors we are supposed to be in the earth.

It shows up when we take an inventory of our lives and realize there are significant pieces not yet matured, and we begin the necessary work of growth and development to make us whole.

It shows up when we develop a ravenous appetite to share the best part of who we are with the world with the intent to make a difference.

It shows up when we realize that what we currently may be doing on our daily jobs, is most likely the very breeding ground of research and development for what we ultimately will be producing with our lives.

It shows up when someone turns to you for help, and you realize that the little that you think you had to offer was the exact amount of all they needed.

It shows up when you arrive at a place and a void is there, and others decide you are the right person who is able to fill that void, and you do.

It shows up when the heart of you who loves to *do* something that you thought you could *never* do but always *imagined* and *hoped* that somehow you *would* do, and God decides that this is the day you will do it.

It shows up as the quintessential core of you recognizes the truest of the gift that God has placed within you, and it rises to the occasion, and the gift prepares itself to make its contribution in the earth.

Then the gift takes its place within you and gives an unprecedented presence to your inner self. Everything else seemingly makes room for this gift, and all of it shifts to a secondary position and yields to a place of humility and servitude. You then have an awareness of who you are and what you possess. Now that the gift has shown up, you undertake a quest to perfect the gift by using it, and the job, such as it is, or your life's environment, suddenly seems like a perfect place to perfect your gift. Then you continue to work the gift until God moves you to the place where the *magnitude of the imagination* of what you saw in your mind's eye can be created. With an understanding that, it is only moments away. For the wait, the delay, was never intended to be, nor was it ever a denial; it was merely the development phase before production, the gestation period before the delivery.

*It shows up in our lives as we become the wandering lost soul looking for our best self within ourselves.*
—Author's Quote

## The Wright Brothers and Their Plane

Orville and Wilbur Wright: The Brothers Who Changed Aviation; here's their biographical recorded success:

> It was twelve seconds that would change the world forever. On the cold, windy morning of December 17, 1903, on the windswept, sandy dunes of Kitty Hawk, North Carolina, a handful of men gathered around a homemade mechanical contraption of wood and fabric. They were there to witness the culmination of years of study, trial and error, sweat, and sacrifice made by two humble, modest men from Dayton, Ohio. That day, the Wright Brothers' dreams of flight would come to fruition as Orville Wright took to the sky for twelve bumpy seconds.
>
> "I like to think about that first airplane, the way it sailed off in the air as pretty as any bird you ever laid your eyes on. I don't think I ever saw a prettier sight in my life," eyewitness John T. Daniels later recalled. Daniels was in awe of Orville and his older brother, Wilbur, whom he called "the workingest boys" he'd ever met in his life. For these two thoughtful bachelor brothers, their years of low-key, methodical research had finally paid off. Always cautious, Orville was shocked at "our audacity in attempting flights in a new and untried machine under such circumstances."
>
> The brothers never attended college. In 1889, while still in high school, Orville started a printing press. Wilbur soon joined him in the venture, and in 1893 the boys opened a bicycle shop they would name the Wright Cycle Company in Dayton, Ohio. Cycling was all the rage, and the brothers were soon designing and fabricating their own bikes
>
> Although they would work and live together until Wilbur's early death, the brothers were not without their individual quirks. According to biographer David McCullough, Wilbur

was more hyper, outgoing, serious and studious—he never forgot a fact and seemed to live in his own head. In contrast, Orville was very shy, but also much happier, with a sunnier outlook on life. He also had a brilliant, mechanically oriented mind.

The brothers became avid bird watchers, studying how they flew. "Learning the secret of flight from a bird was a good deal like learning the secret of magic from a magician," Orville would later say.

The brothers began writing the Smithsonian Institute and the Weather Bureau for information and advice regarding theories of flight and aeronautics. Around the turn of the century, in the back of their booming bike shop, they began to construct their own glider.[33]

## Maya Angelou Most Prominent Poet and More

Maya Angelou's multiplicities' works are discovered in her biographical recorded success:

Considered to be one of the most consequential figures of the twentieth century, Maya Angelou had a diverse career spanning five decades: first as a singer and dancer, then as a journalist and civil-rights activist, and later as a memoirist, poet, and screenwriter.

Here's a look at five monumental achievements of the late Angelou, who died in 2014 at the age of eighty-six:

She was a civil rights activist.

Having traveled the world and met with Malcolm X while living in Ghana, Angelou returned to the United States in 1964 to help the Black leader in his political efforts. However, soon after she arrived stateside, Malcolm X was assassinated. Despite his death, Angelou continued working with the civil rights movement and helped raise funds for Dr. Martin Luther King

Jr. Unfortunately, the young artist found herself devastated once again when Dr. King was murdered on her birthday in 1968. It was during this time that novelist James Baldwin encouraged Angelou to write, and she began work on her groundbreaking memoir *I Know Why the Caged Bird Sings*.

Angelou published *I Know Why the Caged Bird Sings* in 1969, which recalled her childhood experiences growing up in Arkansas and becoming a mother at sixteen. It became an instant bestseller and stayed on the *New York Times* paperback bestseller list for the next two years. Nominated for a National Book Award in 1970, it is considered her most famous work. In 2011, *Time* magazine ranked it as one of the most influential books of modern times.

In 1972 Angelou expanded her writing and musical talents by writing and scoring *Georgia, Georgia*, a Swedish-American drama that would later be nominated for a Pulitzer Prize. She would go on to write for television, theatre, and would eventually reach her goal of directing a film with *Down in the Delta* in 1998.

In 1993 she became the first female inaugural poet in U.S. presidential history when she recited her poem, "On the Pulse of Morning," for President Bill Clinton's inauguration. She became the first African American poet and first female poet to recite her work for a U.S. president's inauguration. The only inaugural poet who came before her was Robert Frost who recited "The Gift Outright" during President John F. Kennedy's ceremony in 1961.

She was awarded the Presidential Medal of Freedom.

After having garnered numerous prestigious literary and humanitarian awards as well as over fifty honorary degrees, Angelou was honored by President Barack Obama, who bestowed the 2010 Presidential Medal of Freedom on her the following year. The Presidential Medal is the highest civilian honor in the United States.[34]

## Mark Zuckerberg the Facebook Mogul

Mark Zuckerberg and his world changing Facebook's success is noted in this biographical sketch:

> Zuckerberg was born on May 14, 1984, in White Plains, New York, into a comfortable, well-educated family. He was raised in the nearby village of Dobbs Ferry. Zuckerberg's father, Edward Zuckerberg, ran a dental practice attached to the family's home. His mother, Karen, worked as a psychiatrist before the birth of the couple's four children — Mark, Randi, Donna, and Arielle.
>
> Zuckerberg developed an interest in computers at an early age. When he was about twelve, he used Atari BASIC to create a messaging program he named "Zucknet." His father used the program in his dental office, so that the receptionist could inform him of a new patient without yelling across the room. The family also used Zucknet to communicate within the house.
>
> Together with his friends, he also created computer games just for fun, yet Zuckerberg remained fascinated by computers and continued to work on developing new programs. While still in high school, he created an early version of the music software Pandora, which he called Synapse. At Harvard he also invented Facemash, which compared the pictures of two students on campus and allowed users to vote on which one was more attractive. The program became wildly popular, but was later shut down by the school administration after it was deemed inappropriate.
>
> Zuckerberg and his friends Dustin Moskovitz, Chris Hughes, and Eduardo Saverin created The Facebook, a site that allowed users to create their own profiles, upload photos, and communicate with other users. The group ran the site out of a dorm room at Harvard University until June 2004. That year Zuckerberg

*dropped out* of college and moved the company to Palo Alto, California. By the end of 2004, Facebook had 1 million users.

In 2005, Zuckerberg's enterprise received a huge boost from the venture capital firm Accel Partners. Accel invested $12.7 million into the network, which at the time was open only to Ivy League students.[35]

**Jeff Bezos and Amazon, the E-commerce Leader**

Jeff Bezos produces a dynasty with Amazon and his success is recorded here:

Bezos was born on January 12, 1964, in Albuquerque, New Mexico, to a teenage mother, Jacklyn Gise Jorgensen, and his biological father, Ted Jorgensen.

Bezos graduated summa cum laude from Princeton University in 1986 with a degree in computer science and electrical engineering. He showed an early interest in how things work, turning his parent's garage into a laboratory and rigging electrical contraptions around his house as a child.

He moved to Miami with his family as a teenager, where he developed a love for computers and graduated as the valedictorian of his high school. It was during high school that he started his first business, the Dream Institute, an educational summer camp for fourth, fifth, and sixth graders.

After graduating from Princeton, Bezos found work at several firms on Wall Street, including Fitel, Bankers Trust, and the investment firm D.E. Shaw. In 1990, Bezos became D.E. Shaw's youngest vice president. His career in finance was extremely lucrative when Bezos chose to make a risky move into the nascent world of e-commerce. He quit his job in 1994, moved to Seattle, and targeted the untapped potential of the Internet market by opening an online bookstore.

On July 16, 1995, Bezos opened Amazon.com, which he'd named after the meandering South American river, after asking 300 friends to beta test his site. In the months leading up to launch, a few employees began developing software with Bezos in his garage. They eventually expanded operations into a two-bedroom house equipped with three Sun Microsystem workstations. The initial success of the company was meteoric. With no press promotion, Amazon.com sold books across the United States and in forty-five foreign countries within thirty days. In two months, sales reached $20,000 a week, growing faster than Bezos and his start-up team had envisioned.

In 1997, Amazon.com went public leading many market analysts to question whether the company could hold its own when traditional retailers launched their own e-commerce sites. Two years later, the start-up not only kept up, but had outpaced competitors, becoming an e-commerce leader.

Bezos continued to diversify Amazon's offerings with the sale of CDs and videos in 1998, and later adding clothes, electronics, toys, and more through major retail partnerships. While many dot-coms of the early '90s went bust, Amazon flourished with yearly sales that jumped from $510,000 in 1995 to over $17 billion in 2011.

As part of Bezos's 2018 annual shareholder letter, the media tycoon said the company had surpassed 100 million paid subscribers for Amazon Prime. By September 2018, Amazon was valued at more than $1 trillion, the second company to ever hit that record just a few weeks after Apple.[36]

**And Chocolate**

It all started in Central America and grew to a phenomenal success seen here:

> Chocolate's 4,000-year history began in ancient Mesoamerica, present day Mexico. It's here that the first cacao plants were found. The Olmec, one of the earliest civilizations in Latin America, were the first to turn the cacao plant into chocolate. They drank their chocolate during rituals and used it as medicine. Their word, kakawa, gave us our word "cacao."
>
> Centuries later, the Mayans praised chocolate as the drink of the gods. Mayan chocolate was a revered brew made of roasted and ground cacao seeds mixed with chilies, water, and cornmeal. Mayans poured this mixture from one pot to another, creating a thick foamy beverage called *xocoatl,* meaning "bitter water."
>
> By the fifteenth century, the Aztecs used cocoa beans as currency. They believed that chocolate was a gift from the god Quetzalcoatl, and drank it as a refreshing beverage, an aphrodisiac, and even to prepare for war.
>
> *Chocolate reaches Spain*
>
> No one knows for sure when chocolate came to Spain. Legend has it that explorer Hernán Cortés brought chocolate to his homeland in 1528. Cortés was believed to have discovered chocolate during an expedition to the Americas. Ostensibly in search of gold and riches, he instead found a cup of cocoa given to him by the Aztec emperor.
>
> When Cortés returned home, he introduced cocoa seeds to the Spanish. Though still served as a drink, Spanish chocolate was mixed with sugar and honey to sweeten the naturally bitter taste. Chocolate quickly became popular among the rich and

wealthy. Even Catholic monks loved chocolate and drank it to aid religious practices.

*Chocolate seduces Europe*

The Spanish kept chocolate quiet for a very long time. It was nearly a century before the treat reached neighboring France and then the rest of Europe. In 1615, French King Louis XIII married Anne of Austria, daughter of Spanish King Phillip III. To celebrate the union, she brought samples of chocolate to the royal courts of France.

Following France's lead, chocolate soon appeared in Britain at special "chocolate houses." As the trend spread through Europe, many nations set up their own cacao plantations in countries along the equator.

*A Chocolate Revolution*

Chocolate remained immensely popular among European aristocracy. Royals and the upper classes consumed chocolate for its health benefits as well as its decadence. Chocolate was still being produced by hand, which was a slow and laborious process. But with the Industrial Revolution around the corner, things were about to change.

In 1828, the invention of the chocolate press revolutionized chocolate making. This innovative device could squeeze cocoa butter from roasted cacao beans, leaving a fine cocoa powder behind. The powder was then mixed with liquids and poured into a mold, where it solidified into an edible bar of chocolate.

And just like that, the modern era of chocolate was born.[37]

*Principle 4—Wait for It . . .*

Each envisioned it, produced it and submitted their contributions to the earth.

*Don't only admire other's lives;
produce something
and
Let them admire yours!
—Author's Quote*

# Ten

## *Principle 5—Be It . . .*

### *It Will Certainly Come*
### *—Habakkuk 2:3 AMP*

---

**Purpose Is Fulfillment**

Living a life of fulfillment is about having a purpose for your life beyond what you do for a living.

Fulfillment; it has come. The *Merriam-Webster Dictionary* defines it as an act or process of delivering a product.[38] All requirements met! A favorable or desired outcome! Accomplishing the intent of the plan! Arriving at or achieving greatness as defined by you! It's the *wow* moment of your life, the thing that makes you joyful, happy, satisfied, that gives you a sense of worth, an added value to your day. Ultimately, fulfillment represents your own measured personal best. Prosperity Purpose.

There comes a time in all of our lives when we define our own sense of prosperity, the thing that gives you that greatest moment of "I always wanted to do that, and now I have," that moment when you say, "I really did that!" the times when you say, "I'm so glad I didn't quit!" especially since you would have been quitting on yourself! But you didn't! These are all success moments! Prosperous moments! These are your moments.

People measure prosperity many different ways. One of the most common ways is by money: how much one can acquire, how many assets one has, the value of your financial portfolio, what's your net worth, and the like. Even our society names the wealthiest people in the world by name and number and then categorizes them by the number of recorded zeros. And if that's all you are looking for, success that is measured by wealth only, perhaps that is good. Yet, what about the many other things by which we measure success that are equally important and conceivably more significant?

What about the goal you set out for your life: to own a house, own some land, travel the world, get married, have your first child, own a business, earn a degree, volunteer in an area of great need. What about a successful entrepreneurship endeavor?

What about the successful recovery from a major surgery, a healthy doctor's report of a condition that was suspicious, family and their welfare and the many other definitions of being prosperous, as defined by the things of your life?

The key is to know that life has a purpose! Life is so much more than existing, just being here, just getting up every day and making our way to a job, even if we absolutely love it. Even spending time with family and friends, enjoying a good meal or anything else that may define a day of your life as indeed meaningful but not necessarily true fulfillment. For those for whom the majority of these may be absolutely wonderful, then you are way ahead of the game. However, this is not the definition of fulfillment. It is only *truly* meaningful when you indeed fulfill your life's purpose!

There is a reason why each of us exists, and it's not just to bring happiness to everyone else's life while inside, you silently suffer because you feel miserable, undervalued or unsatisfied by your own life. Each one of us has a value to add and an intended purpose for being here.

Yes, we often use the expression, "You have to find your purpose," and this is true! We cannot discount that. Nevertheless, we must find it using the steps mentioned in this book.

Otherwise, we can waste a lot of time and effort testing methods that are fruitless in attempts to arrive at it quicker.

Once you started taking an inventory of your life and write down your plans, hopes, dreams, and desires, your mind will start orchestrating for you how to achieve those things. What you have done by putting these things into words is give your mind something to focus on so that energy can then begin to go there and begin to create it. Writing it down will cause you to start gravitating and searching, seeking out the things that can make it happen. Your thoughts create an image for you. We often try to do things by memorization, but memorization is temporary. Imagination, powered by visualization, is endless.

We tend to only memorize things that our subconscious can recall. But if we plan things out by visualization, our minds can continue to create what it is visualizing. We must use our senses to create vision, and that is not to be limited by eyesight only. We must have imaginary vision. What the mind can imagine, it can achieve. Imagination vision has no limitations. It is not dictated by nearsighted vision, farsighted vision, or physical vision at all; it is the mind's vision. You are seeing with your mind's eye.

I am mindful of a very valuable lesson I have learned from a passage of Scripture that says, "and now nothing will be restrained from them, which they have *imagined* to do" (Gen. 11:6 KJV, emphasis added).

Remember as a child, the things that we could imagine being and, in our heart of hearts, we were those things: superheroes, astronauts, teachers, lawyers, even monsters, and animals? We would imitate the behavior, sounds, actions, and even their environment. We were what we saw in our minds.

No one can ever tell you what is in your imagination or that you can't have the things you imagine . . . No one!

Then, we got older, and life happened, and we began to only believe what was told to us, what we experienced, and what we were able to accomplish. We began to believe only the information from our external stimulus, and we stopped listening to our imaginations. We stopped believing that our lives had more of a purpose than the one we were currently living. We started only trying to remember instead of trying to create with an imagination.

We became programmed by society's programming of the ways of life, the social acceptance of what was deemed to be normal, common, traditional, and other nomenclature for life. Mostly what was acceptable included the typical blue-collar/white-collar, professional, career-oriented, artisan, and hourly wage jobs. These standards are fine standards to have; however, they must not be deemed as the only standards to ever have. There is more to your life that you must pursue. You must now become it.

*Living a life of fulfillment*
*is about arriving*
*at the pinnacle of*
*purpose.*
—*Author's Quote*

## Conclusion

# *Purpose* Is Fulfillment

God is the only one qualified to write your life as a business plan, including everything about your life that will ever happen, at the beginning of your life! Your ending was written at your beginning. Don't let life cheat you out of what is already yours; live as the curator of your life. It is a fixed life.

Be confident. Believe in yourself and what you are presenting. Your life has been written as a successful business plan, written by God Himself. His plan for you is designed to bring abundance, wealth, health, love, and joy. *"For I know what I have planned for you,' says the LORD. 'I have plans to prosper you, not to harm you. I have plans to give you a future filled with hope"* (Jeremiah 29:11, NET). Thus, live out your purpose with intent.

Live your life with confidence, certainty, assurance, and determination, and watch the readers of your life who will extrapolate purpose for theirs and follow suit.

And always remember: Your Life *Has* a Purpose!

# Meet the Author

Dr. Leah Cunningham, as an emotional health and wellness educator, has passionately helped many navigate their way through the metamorphosis of life and discover that their *Life Has a Purpose.* Embracing her own metamorphosis through life's experiences, relationships, the corporate world, nursing, ministry, and her military service, she now educates and motivates many individuals on how to live their *best* lives.

Leah's twenty-five-plus years as a combined professional nurse quality manager, compliance officer, Christian educator, empowerment speaker, published author, United States Navy veteran, and ordained minister have given her a wealth of education, experience, and expertise.

Leah is a graduate of the University of Central Florida with a Bachelor's of Science in Nursing. She also holds a National Child Development Associate's Degree awarded from the National Credentialing Program from the Council for Professional Recognition, Washington, D.C. She has an Early Childhood Education Diploma from Stratford Career Institute. Her Masters of Biblical Studies of Christian Education degree is from Dayspring Theological Seminary, Florida, where in appreciation for all of her formal education, numerous years of experience, liberal community contributions, and other submitted published works she was honored with a Doctorate Degree in Christian Education.

Dr. Cunningham's personal experience, education, and expertise have prepared her with an arsenal of tools to be able to evaluate, develop, teach, and train successful emotional health and wellness concepts, allowing those in need to reach their personal and professional career life goals.

Leah is happily married to her husband Rayland, who has been her greatest motivation and accountability partner for finishing this book. She affectionately refers to him as her "hero and king."

*"I have allowed God to merge my life's experiences, my writings, and my formal education for the development of gifts and talents in the areas of emotional healing and wellness, with the ability to educate and motivate many into a better life.*
*I am contributing 'my life's purpose' to the earth"*
*— Author's Personal Note*

To get connected and learn more about Leah Riddick Cunningham and to view her other books such as, *"Bad Memories Sabotage Healthy Emotions"* visit her website:

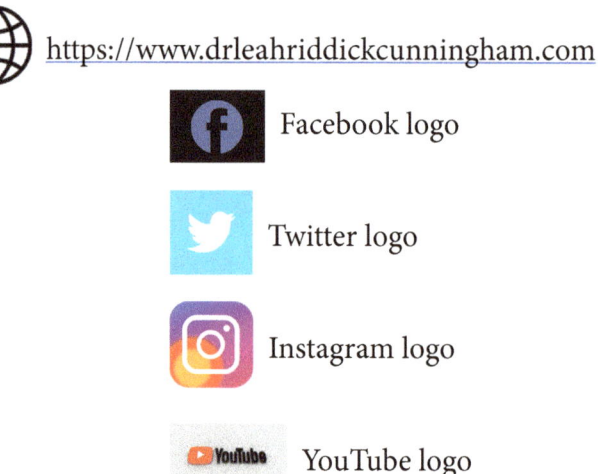

https://www.drleahriddickcunningham.com

Facebook logo

Twitter logo

Instagram logo

YouTube logo

# *Endnotes*

1. Brian Hill, Difference Between Executive Summary & Introduction, accessed January 26, 2019, https://bizfluent.com/info-8210984-difference-between-executive-summary-introduction.html.

2. Oxford Learners Dictionary.com Dictionary, s.v. "purpose" accessed January 8, 2019, https://www.oxfordlearnersdictionaries.com/us/definition/english/purpose?q=purpose.

3. John Allen Saunders, "Life is what happens to us while we are making other plans" accessed January 8, 2019, https://en.wikipedia.org/wiki/Allen_Saunders#.

4. John Lennon, "Life is what happens to you while you're busy making other plans." accessed January 8, 2019, https://quotepark.com/quotes/1851325-john-lennon-life-is-what-happens-to-you-while-youre-busy-maki/.

5. Holman Bible Publishers, (Copyright c 1991) "Image of God", accessed January 8, 2019, http://mercury.webster.edu/kindt3/aicourse/imageofgod.htm.

6. Sharon Daloz Parks, "How Life Purpose Evolves", University of Minnesota, accessed February 15, 2019, https://www.takingcharge.csh.umn.edu/what-life-purpose.

7. Arthur Masloski, "Goldfish: Myths Debunked" *Tropical Fish Magazine*, January 2009, accessed February 10, 2019 https://www.tfhmagazine.com/articles/freshwater/goldfish-myths-debunked#:~:text.

b. Phil Ritchie, "Do goldfish really grow to the size of their tank?" *Cosmos and The Science of Everything,* September 2016, accessed February 10, 2019 https://cosmosmagazine.com/nature/do-goldfish-really-grow-to-the-size-of-their- tank/#:~:text.

c. Lindsey Stanton, "Goldfish CAN Grow to the Size of Their Tank" *Goldfish Tank Size Guide & Why It's Not Important as You Think,* accessed February 10, 2019, https://www.itsafishthing.com/goldfish-tank-size/.

## Chapter 1

8   Medline Plus, "Are fingerprints determined by genetics?", accessed January 21, 2020 https://medlineplus.gov/genetics/understanding/traits/fingerprints/.

b. Glenn Langenburg, "Are one's fingerprints similar to those of his or her parents in any discernable way?" *Scientific American,* January 2005, accessed January 21, 2020, (quote emphasis & edited by Leah Riddick Cunningham-author) https://www.scientificamerican.com/article/are-ones-fingerprints-sim/#:~:text.

## Chapter 2

9   Merriam-Webster.com Dictionary, s.v. "belong," accessed March 3 2021,

10  James Chen, *Investopedia*. Medium of Exchange Definition accessed March 2021 https://www.investopedia.com/terms/m/mediumofexchange.asp#:~:text.

## Chapter 3

11  Merriam-Webster.com Dictionary, s.v. "selfishness," accessed May 3, 2020, https://www.merriam-webster.com/dictionary/selfishness.

## Chapter 6

12  Bible Hub, Strong's Exhaustive Concordance, "chazon: vision" = mental sight, accessed February 2020, https://biblehub.com/hebrew/2377.htm.

13  Medline Plus, "Visual acuity test", accessed June 2020

https://medlineplus.gov/ency/article/003396.htm#:~:text.

14  Teresa Bergen, Judith Marcin, M.D. "Farsightedness", *Healthline*, May 2017, accessed June 2020, https://www.healthline.com/health/farsightedness.

15  Miller-Keane Encyclopedia and Dictionary of Medicine, Nursing, and Allied Health, Seventh Edition. s.v. "myopia." accessed June 2020 from https://medical-dictionary.thefreedictionary.com/myopia.

b.  Whitney Seltman, OD, "Peripheral Vision Loss: Causes and Treatments," *WebMD*, accessed June 5, 2020 https://www.webmd.com/eye-health/common-causes-peripheral-vision-loss.

16  Merriam-Webster.com Dictionary, s.v. "tunnel vision," accessed May 2020, https://www.merriam-webster.com/dictionary/tunnel%20vision.

17  Merriam-Webster.com Dictionary, s.v. "mind's eye," accessed June 2020, https://www.merriam-webster.com/dictionary/mind%27s%20eye.

18  Christopher Bergland, The "Right Brain" Is Not the Only Source of Creativity- 11 brain areas in four hemispheres create a "mental workspace" of imagination, September 2013, accessed Jan 2021

19  Kendra Cherry, "An Overview of Aphantasia", *verywell mind* accessed Jan 2020, https://www.verywellmind.com/aphantasia-overview-4178710#:~:text.

20  Anna Clemens, "When the Mind\'s Eye Is Blind" SCIENTIFIC AMERICAN, a *Division of Springer Nature America, Inc,* updated Aug 2018, accessed Jan 2020 https://www.scientificamerican.com/article/when-the-minds-eye-is-blind1/.

21  A. Zeman; M. Dewar; Sala S. Della; Lives without imagery–Congenital aphantasia. Cortex. 2015;73:378–380. doi:10.1016/j.cortex.2015.05.019.

22  Miller-Keane Encyclopedia and Dictionary of Medicine, Nursing, and Allied Health, Seventh Edition. s.v. "tunnel vision." accessed June 2020 from https://medical-dictionary.thefreedictionary.com/tunnel+vision.

23  Merriam-Webster.com Dictionary, s.v. "tunnel vision," accessed May 2020, https://www.merriam-webster.com/dictionary/tunnel%20vision.

24  Walt Disney -https://historicmissourians.shsmo.org/walt-disney.

25  Shirley-Ann Jackson–https://biography.yourdictionary.com/shirley-ann-jackson; https://www.yesmagazine.org/health-happiness/2016/03/21/10-black-women-innovators-and-the-awesome-things-they-brought-us.

26  Marie Van Brittan Brown -https://timeline.com/marie-van-brittan-brown-b63b72c415f0; https://thinkgrowth.org/14-black-inventors-you-probably-didnt-know-about-3c0702cc63d2.

27  Sandra Sealey, "Home security on Brown's mind", *Nation News*, February 2019 references '2016 edition New Scientist, 100 million concealed closed-circuit cameras now in operation worldwide' https://www.nationnews.com/2019/02/22/home-security-on-browns-mind/.

28   Malala Yousafzai (aka Malala) https://matterapp.com/blog/what-is-servant-leadership-and-why-its-important#:~:text.

## Chapter 7

29   Nicole Beasley, "Difference Between Eidetic Memory and Photographic Memory", *Better Help*, https://www.betterhelp.com/advice/memory/difference-between-eidetic-memory-and-photographic-memory/.

30   Siobhan Kelleher Kukolic, "The average person has between 12,000 and 60,000thoughts per day", June 2018, https://siobhankukolic.com/the-average-person-has-between-12000-and-60000-thoughts-per-day.

31   Expressive writing, https://www.psychologytoday.com/us/blog/write-yourself-well/201208/expressive-writing

## Chapter 8

32   Bernard Mokua, "5 Ways To Create Momentum In Business", *Self Made Success*, Oct 2015, accessed June 2018, http://selfmadesuccess.com/how-to-create-unstoppable-momentum-in-business/.

## Chapter 9

33   Orville and Wilbur Wright, https://www.biography.com/news/orville-wilbur-wright-brothers-first-flight.

34   Maya Angelou, https://www.biography.com/writer/maya-angelou.

35   Mark Zuckerberg, https://www.biography.com/business-figure/mark-zuckerberg.

36  Jeff Bezo, https://www.biography.com/business-figure/jeff-bezo.

37  Chocolate, https://www.history.com/topics/ancient-americas/history-of-chocolate.

   Chocolate, https://www.magnumicecream.com/us/en/stories/food/the-history-of-chocolate.html.

   Chocolate, https://www.smithsonianmag.com/history/archaeology-chocolate-180954243/.

Chapter 10

38  Merriam-Webster.com Dictionary, s.v. "fulfillment," accessed June 4, 2020, https://www.merriam-webster.com/dictionary/fulfillment.

CPSIA information can be obtained
at www.ICGtesting.com
Printed in the USA
BVHW012111310123
657545BV00014B/182